MW01221994

EXPOSING
FALSEHOOD

AN EXAMINATION OF PUBLIC DECEPTION

Issues worth investigating amid confusion and uncertainty.

EXPOSING FALSEHOOD

AN EXAMINATION OF PUBLIC DECEPTION

Issues worth investigating amid confusion and uncertainty.

Michael Uhryn

EXPOSING FALSEHOOD
An Examination of Public Deception

Copyright © Michael Uhryn, 2019

Published by Michael Uhryn, Edmonton, Canada

ISBN   0-978-1-77354-179-2 Print
          0-978-1-77354-182-2 eBook

Publication assistance and digital printing in Canada by

PUBLISHING
PageMaster.ca

This book is dedicated to all my friends, who in their own way, are promoting a better world and a brighter future.

Table of Contents

Prologue

The world is in a state of turmoil, confusion and uncertainty. We can count our blessings so far for not experiencing a global nuclear apocalypse or an environmental disaster; however, the warning signs of nuclear or environmental catastrophe is still before us. Resolution of the two issues mentioned are critical for human survival. Power structures, operating under the guise of neoliberalism, dominating the governments of most modern societies are a major obstacle and threat to resolving the two existential threats facing humanity.

The Canadian composite power structure, invisible and ghost-like, which consists of business tycoons, banks, military, police, secret service, higher echelons of religious authorities and corporate media, is intertwined with the power structures of other nations. Major players of different power structures collectively dominate domestic and world issues.

Canadian society is confronted with many important secondary issues overshadowed by two critical issues known as existential threats – climate change and threat of nuclear war. There are other issues worthy of analysis, careful examination and scrutiny. Ordinary Canadians, whether they be working men and women, farmers or students, are daily bombarded with a corporate ideological slant and bias on all important issues. The corporate media, an integral part of the Canadian power structure, conveys and reinforces the message that serves the

interest of the corporate elite, i.e. the 1% of population that con-
centrates its wealth at the top of the pyramid. Such issues as
human nature, unemployment, poverty, alienation or war are
presented, interpreted and propagandized in the interest of the
ideology of the Canadian power structure and corporate elite.

In this book, a number of serious issues will be examined and
presented from the point of view and interest of the vast majority of Canadian people, who are wage earners and ordinary folk,
as opposed to the 1% who derive huge profits and amass wealth.
It's not enough to expose the public to ideas propagated and propagandized only by the corporate media; in a truthful and more
substantive democracy, it's necessary to counter and balance the
corporate message with ideas which reflect the interest of the
majority of ordinary folk and wage earners. Clearly, in Canadian
democracy, it is critical that people have the opportunity to
examine ideas thoughtfully from different perspectives if they
are to arrive at an intelligent and positive decision. Hopefully,
this book will succeed to some extent in exposing the many
fallacies that have permeated the ideas and fabric of Canadian
society.

CHAPTER 1

Enigma of Human Nature

The starting point for obtaining truthful knowledge that explains the profound conflicts and confusion in Canadian society, and for that matter globally, necessarily requires a better understanding of "human nature".

Presently, in Canadian society and the Western world, a daily and constant bombardment is maintained, portraying the negative and bestial behaviour and nature of human beings. The corporate media persists in characterizing human beings as selfish, egotistical and greedy. A strong tendency exists nowadays to resurrect Thomas Hobbes (1588-1679), who, in his book *Leviathan*, states that life for humans in a state of nature was "solitary, poor, nasty, brutish and short." It's understandable why Thomas Hobbes arrived at such a view on human nature, since he lived during turbulent times—the period of the English civil war (1642-1651). His psychological theory that man is inherently selfish, egotistic and motivated by selfish desires was largely the outcome of the conditions experienced by Thomas Hobbes. However, there is no anthropological evidence to support his position on human nature.

It's important to grasp the significance of the political implication arising from the view adopted by Thomas Hobbes. According to Hobbes, if man existed alone there would be no problem; however, when groups get together, conflict and confusion inevitably transpire over their selfish desires. In an effort to survive and have stability, Hobbes puts forth the political and philosophical argument that a sovereign, absolute monarchy—a leviathan—necessarily must be established. Indeed, the British monarchy used the arguments of Hobbes to justify their rule.

Interestingly, a different view on human nature was developed by John Locke (1632-1704),[1] who is considered to be the founder of classical liberalism and Western democracy (see his *Second Treatise of Civil Government*). In theory, Locke is diametrically opposed to the psychological view held by Hobbes on human nature. According to Locke's psychological theory, people in general in the state of nature live in harmony; they cooperate with each other and, at times, work for the good of others.[1] Unfortunately, Locke's equivocation on man's behaviour in society as being somewhat good and bad transformed his view on human nature into the realm of ambiguity and uncertainty.

In contrast to Hobbes on primitive life, Jean-Jacques Rousseau (1712-1778) believed that humans in earlier times were "noble savages". According to Rousseau, humans are naturally good, but it's "civilization" that turns them into a "beast."[2] While John Locke viewed the emerging market economy (embryonic capitalism) and technology as positive development, Rousseau argued that modern man should revert to a more "natural" life rather than be engulfed in "technological" living.

Canadian society characterizes man as an ego-centric being with a thirst for dominance and material aggrandizement. The corporate media with its one-sided, calculated, twisted, slanted and negative daily message on human behaviour, creates the image in the minds of ordinary folk that they are selfish egotistical, greedy and aggressive. Violence and ills in society, conflicts and wars we are witnessing today, as perceived and orches-

---

1   Locke, John. *Second Treatise of Civil Government*. p. 11-13.

2   Rousseau, Jean-Jacques. *The Essential Writings of Rousseau*.

trated by corporate media, are the consequence of man's innate depravity and his brutal nature. It's interesting to note the countless positive and beautiful deeds performed by people in everyday life largely ignored and rarely expressed by corporate media. Nowadays, many scholars and writers tend to express a positive view of human nature but are often denied access to the media. Analysis and careful scrutiny tell us that corporate media promotes gross negativity on human nature intentionally, in a calculated mode. It's unfortunate that the Canadian power structure uses the corporate media to popularize and propagandize the despicable nature of man in society.

Power structures of the Western world seek to sustain their political power in society by continuing to permeate the minds of ordinary folk with a false image of human nature. Human beings are socially and psychologically conditioned to accept an economic system which pits man against man. People succumb to the capitalist system, not because they agree with its means and ends, but because they are made to feel they have no choice. Workers conform under the economic system, because they have too much to lose by challenging authorities in the workplace. The Western world, under the guise of neoliberalism, adheres to the dictum stated by Adam Smith in his book *The Wealth of Nations*, published in 1776. In it, he states the invisible hand is an unobservable force, which helps the demand and supply of goods in a free market to reach equilibrium automatically.[3] Without the invisible hand, society would descend into life suggested by Thomas Hobbes as "solitary, brutish, nasty and short." Over time, the emerging capitalist economy and neoliberalism was to solidify the negative nature of man.

Neither John Locke, Jacque Rousseau nor Adam Smith were able to foresee the impact new social and economic conditions would have in shaping their understanding of human nature.

---

3   Smith, Adam. *The Wealth of Nations*. University of Chicago. p. 477.

The rising merchant class, which was becoming a viable embryonic capitalist class, was to carry the day in determining how human nature was to unfold and be interpreted in the Western world. It wasn't until the 19th, 20th and 21st centuries, with the ascension of new authors and writers such as Karl Marx, Herbert Marcuse, Paul Sartre, Eric Fromm, Albert Camus and others that a different disclosure and interpretation was to evolve on human nature. One of the better accounts of a Marxist view on human nature was provided by Erich Fromm in his book *Marx's Concept of Man*, first published in 1961.[4] According to Marx as interpreted by Fromm, there are two types of human drives or desires: firstly, we have the fixed or constant drives as exemplified by hunger and sexual drive, which are an "inherent" part of human nature. These drives can only be modified, accentuated or repressed by conditions of respective cultures. Secondly, we have the "relative appetites or desires" which are "not inherently" tied to human nature, but rather owe their total existence to economic, social and cultural conditions in society.

Although great strides have been made in science, so far, no evidence has been disclosed indicating that man's "relative desires" are inherently connected to human nature. On the contrary, overwhelming evidence and scientific observation points in the direction that man's undesirable behaviour is the result of man being exposed to a negative and dehumanizing socialization and psychological process. Human behaviour characterized by such features as greed and selfishness, lust for political power and money, sexual misconduct and violence, aggressiveness and war, are instilled and reinforced by cultural forces—in particular, by the corporate media in society.

Nevertheless, despite the current widespread negative view of human nature, there is some hope in the world as people are

---

4   Fromm, Eric. *Marx's Concept of Man*. New York: Frederick Ungar Publishing Co. p. 25-26.

searching to find ways of establishing conditions for positive and acceptable behaviour. One shining example of people embarked on the road to developing a cooperative society expressing human nature in a positive way is Mon Dragon Corporation in the Basque region of Spain. Economic and social relations in Mon Dragon are diametrically opposed to the conflictual relations as practised under capitalist organization.

Mon Dragon consists of many cooperative enterprises, accommodating 85,000 members and consisting of four areas: industry, finance, retail and knowledge.[5] In each enterprise, worker members of the co-op own collectively and guide the enterprise.

What Mon Dragon illustrates is that human beings working in a cooperative form of economic and social organization over time would psychologically abandon the Hobbesian notion of human greed and selfishness. Individuals with idealistic and humanistic aspirations would likely turn to Mon Dragon, which is a shining economic and social model to follow. Eliminating or curtailing the clout of a power structure, which directs the corporate media to systematically distort and propagandize human nature in a negative way, is a challenge facing Canada, the Western world and the global community.

Reversing the current pervasive negative trend on human nature, perpetrated and perpetuated by power structures and corporate medias, has become more complicated by the role and impact of religion. Higher echelons of religious authorities of different denominations work closely with power structures and corporate medias to cultivate a negative view of human nature. It's outside the scope of this paper to examine in detail the role religion plays in shaping human nature; suffice to say, that religion characterizing man as being sinful complements the work

---

5   Wolff, Richard. *Capitalism's Crisis Deepens*. Haymarket Books, 2016.

of power structures and corporate medias in promoting the negative view of human nature.

Reversing the current negative trend of human nature in Canadian society is unthinkable without emergence and growth of a viable populace grassroots movement. Development of such a movement, spearheaded by an experienced, progressive and dedicated leadership, is a necessary condition if the entrenched power structure is to be seriously challenged and curtailed in society. It is crucial for the grassroots movement to project a positive view of human nature, as well as a thoughtful economic and social program which caters to the majority of people—ordinary folk and wage-earners. Projection of a populace movement would weaken and degrade the elements of the power structure. By curbing the strength of the power structure and its corporate media, a grass roots movement would be nicely positioned to champion the positive version of human nature. The foundation will have been laid for the populace movement to take a major step in building an egalitarian society,[6] similar to the path laid out by Mon Dragon.

---

6   An egalitarian society is one which provides equal rights and opportunities for all people—political, economic, social, cultural—regardless of race, gender or creed.

CHAPTER 2

Poverty in Canada

The issue of poverty in Canada has been examined by various agencies, anti-poverty groups and officials, including politicians and economists. They look at the issue of poverty extensively and seemingly fail to reach any conclusion as to why poverty exists in Canada. It would appear the issue is too complex and beyond comprehension, or perhaps there is an unwillingness on the part of investigators and analysts to unravel the truth. It's somewhat strange and unfortunate, that with today's advanced technology, ordinary and common folk are still denied a clear explanation on the underlying cause of poverty in Canada. It is the view of a number of scholarly analysts that the issue of poverty is not a mystery and can be clearly explained; however, there is a reluctance to reveal the real cause of poverty partly because of job security considerations.

Before we turn to examine Canadian poverty, it's proper and advisable to state a few relevant facts. It is a statistical fact that Canada's population hovers around 39 million. China's population is estimated to be around 1.3 billion. When examining Canadian poverty analytically, it's useful to compare how the two diverse nations view and cope with poverty. It's important to keep in mind that Canada is the second largest country in the world, larger than China, and endowed with immense natural resources. Interestingly, in 2018, China claimed to have taken

600 million people out of abject poverty. So why can Canada not eliminate poverty?

Taking Canada's wealth and supply of resources into account, it becomes abundantly clear that a disproportionate number of Canadians are unnecessarily experiencing various aspects of poverty. Poverty is widespread in Canada, and according to Statistics Canada (2018), there are 4.9 million (1 in 7) Canadians living in poverty. Income inequality—the gap between the rich and poor—is widening in Canada. According to Canadian Poverty Institute, there is a growing trend of Canadians who live precariously from paycheque to paycheque and are on the edge of falling into an abyss of poverty.[7]

Poverty transcends all age groups and ethnicities in Canadian society. However, it is a troubling revelation, as reported by Canadian Poverty Institute, that Indigenous people in Canada experience the highest levels of poverty. A shocking 1 in 4 Indigenous people—First Nations, Metis and Inuit—are living in poverty, and 4 in 10 Indigenous children live in poverty.[8]

Equally disturbing is the number of single mothers with low incomes, experiencing poverty conditions as they bring up their children. Also of deep concern are people with disabilities or those suffering from mental or physical illness, who are exposed to conditions of poverty and are provided with bare sustenance.

Another distinct group that should not be overlooked are the seniors in Canadian society. If, for one reason or another, a careful plan for retirement was neglected, it may well mean the senior will be confronted by the ugly head of poverty. A Canadian pension and subsidy will provide them with sustenance, but they will still be a victim of impoverishment and poverty. Poverty has a severe negative impact on all age groups;

7   https://www.povertyinstitute.ca/poverty-canada

8   Ibid.

however, there is ample evidence indicating that poverty tends to impact seniors the hardest.

Of great concern are the children of Canada, for they represent the future of the country. According to Canadian Poverty Institute, there are 1.34 million children in Canada living in poverty.[9] It's a disgrace and shame in this day and age, when Canadian governments have such immense resources at their disposal, that 1 in 5 Canadian children live in abject poverty.

What does poverty do to children? What are the negative impacts of poverty on children?

It is sad and humiliating when so many of our children take jobs to help their parents when the family is in economic distress. Children assisting their parents financially is an honourable gesture and activity; however, it has a negative impact on their schoolwork and educational achievement. It is vile and inhumane when impoverished children are denied full advantage of learning and other opportunities. It's important to point out that parents living in poverty often minimize the impacts of poverty on their children by sacrificing their own economic needs, activities and lifestyle. However, such parental action, lofty and noble as it may appear, is likely to precipitate serious financial, mental, and relationship problems, including substance abuse; this can affect parental behaviour and cause negative impacts on physical and mental health of children. There is an abundance of evidence strongly suggesting a significant correlation between children's early cognitive and educational development and attaining future jobs with a livable and decent wage.

Many scholars agree that poverty imposes negative effects on the child's health and social, emotional, cognitive, behavioural and educational outcomes. In short, poverty degrades the child, thwarts development of the child's potential, destroys

---

9   Ibid.

the child's self esteem and ultimately sets the child on a path of estrangement and alienation.

What is the answer? How can we cut off the negative head of poverty?

Why is there poverty in Canadian society? What is the root cause(s) of poverty?

There exists an enormous amount of literature on poverty; however, when it comes to determining the root cause(s) of poverty, there appears to be massive uncertainty and confusion. The Canadian power structure, having the corporate media at its disposal, propagandizes and reinforces the neoliberal ideological viewpoint that there will always be a section of Canadians at the pyramidal bottom, living in poverty. However, the corporate media tends to mitigate the severity of poverty on behalf of neoliberalism, anticipating a favourable public reaction. The encouraging part is that many scholars and ordinary Canadians are beginning to seriously question the rationale of neoliberalism on poverty.[10] It's rather disconcerting that neoliberalism is averse to examining the root cause of poverty with the aspiration of eliminating it.

To get at the root cause of poverty, it's necessary to observe how the Canadian economic system operates. It's critical to examine closely how the profit-motive and market economy function. Careful observation of the market economy tells us that poverty in Canadian society is built-in—an inherent feature of the economy.[11] Under the current economic institutional

---

10   Neoliberalism says that human well-being can best be served by allowing entrepreneurs, within the institutional framework, strong property rights, free markets, free trade and as little government intervention as possible in the market economy.

11   A market economy is characterized by productivity for profit, involving a monetary exchange of commodities and services regulated by supply and demand.

framework, entrepreneurs have the constitutional right to set up a business. An established business engages in the production of commodities or services to attain profit, which leads to accumulation of capital and creation of jobs. However, the operation of the Canadian market economy isn't that smooth; the economy has its ups and downs and is entrapped by the business cycle. Every so often, there is downward activity in the economy, characterized as a slump, which means that workers are laid off and widespread unemployment ensues, causing extensive poverty. The demand for labour fluctuates in a market economy; it rises or falls with changes in the business cycle. Notwithstanding the business cycle, the market economy is confronted with a fundamental economic contradiction. An exorbitant amount of wealth and capital tends to be concentrated at the apex of the economic pyramid, causing a great impact on declining purchasing power below. The inevitable result of the economic process is that deep and extensive poverty emerges in Canadian society.

The unrestricted market economy, faced with widening inequality, recurring business cycles and the undesirable concentration of capital at the top, is unquestionably the root cause of poverty in Canada. It's mind-boggling to understand how the capitalist market economy, which is endorsed by neoliberalism, has the capacity to provide an abundance of material commodities and services but is unable to reconcile this abundance with the needs of people.

Canadian market economy appears to have insurmountable difficulty in assuring Canadians of full employment in effort to minimize poverty. It should be pointed out that competition and new technology exacerbates living conditions for workers and people. In a market economy competition gives rise to mergers of companies, which results in laying off workers. Moreover, competition gives corporations no choice but to increase productivity by introducing new equipment, sacrificing workers' employment in the process. Labour - saving technology necessarily eliminates jobs for many people. A close scrutiny of Canadian market economy tells us that an inherent tendency exists within the economy to lay off workers, take workers out of production and likely drive them towards poverty. Regardless of conditions in the economy, the pool of workers who are unemployed, tends to propel wages and benefits to a lower level in the direction of poverty. It is indisputable that the pool of unemployed and countless impoverished workers is the pivot upon which the law of supply and demand rides. It should be emphasized that in a global capitalist market economy, of which Canada is a part, unemployment is profitable in that unemployment lowers wages which are considered to be costs in a market economy.

Before we conclude the chapter by suggesting what might be a workable solution to lowering the level of poverty, or possibly eliminating it, it's advisable to give some attention to what poverty is costing Canadians. It seems ironic and strange to view impoverishment as being a cost factor. However, the harsh reality is that poverty is one of the largest financial burdens imposed on healthcare, criminal justice and economic systems in Canada. Canadians aren't aware of the fact that the cost of the healthcare system is a reflection of poverty. People living in poverty are victims of serious health problems; for example, those victimized by poverty are more likely to develop diabetes and other health problems such as blindness and cardiovascular disease.

According to Canada Without Poverty in 2011, the federal government of Canada spent $19.9 billion alone on employment insurance benefits, while the cost of the Canadian healthcare system was estimated at an additional $7.6 billion. Moreover, in 2011, the federal government spent an estimated $11.2 billion on social assistance.[12]

It would appear that Canada is in a financial poverty quagmire, which will require extraordinary commitment to meet the challenge and place Canada on a good footing.

---

12   www.cwp-csp.ca/poverty/the-cost-of-poverty

What is the solution to decreasing or possibly eliminating poverty in Canada?

As mentioned in the introductory part of the chapter, Canada is the second largest country in the world, endowed with enormous resources. It baffles the human mind why a relatively small population (roughly 39 million people) seems to be bogged down and unable to build an egalitarian society, free of the dreaded curse of poverty. Are Canadians destined to live with poverty indefinitely? Do we not have people with the necessary skills and knowledge to come to grips with the issue of poverty in Canada?

There is a growing number of Canadian scholars who subscribe to the view that any reduction or elimination of poverty in Canada necessitates careful examination and commitment to fully removing the fundamental cause of poverty (i.e. liquidation of the inherent economic contradiction in society). It's inconceivable that the issue of poverty can be resolved without the implementation of many changes in the economy, including major structural reforms. Such economic issues as capital gains tax, tax loopholes, rate of profit and a growing concentration of wealth needs to be examined and acted on. It's incomprehensible and baffling to try grasping the amount of wealth and power that's concentrated in such corporate entities as drug companies; insurance, banking and armaments industries; or multinational oil corporations. Undoubtedly, draconian measures are likely to be exercised in effort to curb or curtail and contain any further concentration of wealth by the business tycoons, who are the cornerstone of the Canadian power structure and market

economy.[13] Working towards an egalitarian society necessarily
requires adoption of a new mode of production and distribution
of commodities; it means workers assuming more control of
industry and working cooperatively in the form of worker self-
directed enterprises (WSDEs). Unlike the inherent feature of
the Canadian market economy, where shareholders and boards
of directors make all important decisions, workers would make
key decisions in self-directed enterprises, regarding what is to
be produced, how it's to be produced, where production is to take
place and what is to be done with profit.[14] Such an organizational
transition necessitates emergence of a viable grassroots movement, which will likely entail a broad section of people from all
walks of life. Nobody has a crystal ball to forecast when such a
movement will appear on the Canadian scene; however, a strong
case can be made that the emergence of such a social movement
is a necessary and sufficient condition for the resolution of the
Canadian poverty dilemma.

---

13   Canadian power structure can best be characterized as a composite and
invisible power structure; it is composite because it's composed of a number of
intertwined distinct elements: business tycoons, banks, military, police force,
secret service, high echelons of religious bodies and corporate media. Power
structure being invisible means it operates behind the scenes as a ghost-like
entity.

14   For a more detailed description of WSDEs, see Capitalism's Crisis Deepens
by Richard Wolff.

CHAPTER 3

The Plight of Indigenous Peoples in Canada

Non-indigenous Canadians celebrated their 150th birthday as a nation with glowing fanfare and enthusiasm in 2017; however, there was a more dormant, cool and less exciting celebration among Indigenous peoples—First nations, Metis and Inuit. Corporate and social medias extolled the event as a great historic moment in the evolution of Canadian democracy, but it paid little attention to the plight of Indigenous peoples during the past 150 years. Relationships between the non-indigenous and Indigenous peoples during the past century and half can hardly be described as amicable, cooperative, Christian and democratic. On numerous occasions, treaties were violated, often leaving people exposed to intolerable living conditions. Indigenous people were systematically disenfranchised, dispossessed, exploited and relegated to the margins of society. At the present time, Indigenous peoples are looking with great expectation for the attainment of self-determination.

With the release of the final document by the Truth Reconciliation Commission (TRC) in 2015, a milestone has been reached in Canadian Indigenous history. The report may well represent a breakthrough in real reconciliation, as well as a positive indication that Indigenous peoples—First Nations, Metis and Inuit—are on the road to complete their journey in the long overdue struggle for self-determination. It appears that the Canadian government and non-indigenous people have taken a significant step in trying to come to terms in understanding and appreciating the depth, magnificence and wonder of Indigenous culture. Should non-indigenous people in Canada make a greater effort to engage in truthful and sincere dialogue with Indigenous peoples, and in the process try to understand their values and culture, amazing and positive outcomes may occur in alleviating poverty among Indigenous communities. It's shocking news, as revealed by Canadian Poverty Institute, to hear that Indigenous people in Canada experience the highest levels of poverty. According to the Institute, an appalling 1 in 4 Indigenous peoples live in poverty.[15] The reality of poverty in these communities tells us that all levels of government need to address the issue of poverty—not with empty words, but with concrete action.

Historically, Indigenous peoples led a relatively peaceful life; their economies were subsistence-oriented—organized around activities involving fishing, hunting and food gathering. It's in this economic and social context that Indigenous peoples were able to develop a rich and unique culture. One of the more important features of Indigenous culture is potlatch, which is largely unknown and a mystery to non-indigenous people. Potlatch is a gift-awarding festival practised by many Indigenous people. Potlatch literally means to make a ceremonial gift at such important events as marriages, births and deaths; all these activities were potlatch occasions. It's noteworthy to mention that events of less importance were also occasions of potlatch, because the basic purpose of potlatch was not the occasion itself, but the establishment of claims to social rank. The potlatch ceremony (Sundance) was usually set for midsummer, at which time the bands and tribes would gather at a designated place.

---

15   https://www.povertyinstitute.ca/poverty-canada

Viewing the cultural dimension of Indigenous people would be incomplete if we were negligent in examining their religious and spiritual life. Spirituality among Indigenous peoples varies widely, as do cultural practices of contemporary Indigenous peoples of Canada.

It's important to mention that Indigenous creation stories often described the origin of the universe, moon, sun and stars as well as the origin of human beings. The creation narratives were to provide education to people on environment, the planetary system, their relationship to the world, as well as the interconnection between them. Many Indigenous peoples believe in a creator, great spirit or great mystery—an omnipotent power that was responsible for creating the world and all things inside. Even more so, the great spirit is found in all living and natural things as well as in places of ritual importance. Such ritual objects as rattles, drums, masks, medicine wheels, medicine bundles and ritual sanctuaries are all imbued with spiritual power. It should be emphasized that the Indigenous communal, traditional way of life—hunting, fishing and food-gathering—was inextricably connected with their religion and spirituality. Finally, various Indigenous oral narratives describe humans making contact with extra-terrestrial beings and the world beyond.

While Indigenous peoples lived according to their culture for many centuries, a new historical period was to unfold in Canada, having a serious and negative impact on the Indigenous peoples. After the Seven Years' War (1756-1763), a war fought between two imperial powers—Britain and France—the territory of New France was placed under British colonial rule. The population of the British colony increased substantially, so that by 1867, there emerged a demand in the British colony for uniting four provinces into a confederation known as the Dominion of Canada.

What impact did the formation of the Dominion of Canada have on the Indigenous peoples?

The new Conservative government of Sir John A. MacDonald made a dramatic departure from King George III's Royal Proclamation of 1763, where he stated all lands remain property of Indigenous peoples unless they are ceded or sold, saying Indigenous people "should not be molested or disturbed" in the quest for territory.[16]

In 1867, under the BNA Act, Section 91(24), the MacDonald government enacted legislation which provided exclusive legislative authority over "Indians, and lands reserved for the Indians." The Act terminated the nation-to-nation relationship and set the conditions for the notorious Indian Act of 1876, which officially brought in colonialism and enforced assimilation.[17]

In an attempt to assimilate the Indigenous peoples into the Anglo-Saxon/Canadian way of life, the MacDonald government embarked upon implementation of brutal, racist and genocidal policies. As part of assimilation policy, the federal government banned the potlatch practice from 1884-1951 by an amendment to the Indian Act.[18] The federal government of the day and its supporters viewed the potlatch ceremony as anti-Christian, cruel and wasteful in property. Since Confederation, both Conservative and Liberal regimes argued that realistic assimilation could only be achieved by abolishing Indigenous cultural practices. Under the Indian Act, engaging in the practise of the potlatch—which encompassed many other ceremonies—was a criminal offence. A rather interesting post-Confederation argument advanced, stating that if potlatch, being the cornerstone of Indigenous culture, could be eradicated, the governments and missionaries would have an unparalleled opportunity to replace the suppressed Indigenous culture with Christianity.

---

16   *New Trail.* Volume 73.1, Spring 2017. University of Alberta. p. 21.

17   Ibid. p. 21.

18   Ibid. p. 21.

It's sad, humiliating and disconcerting that in the many years of potlatch law, an entire generation of Indigenous peoples grew up inhumanely deprived of the cultural fabric of their ancestors. What led Sir John A. MacDonald to say in the House of Commons in 1883 that "Indians" were "savages"?[19] Furthermore, he stated in the same year to Parliament that if Indigenous children were left in the family home, they would "remain savages". Continuing the racist policies, in 1920, Duncan Campbell Scott, Minister of Indian Affairs, speaking to a parliamentary committee, stated "our object is to continue until there is not a single Indian in Canada that has not been absorbed into the body politic."[20]

It's disheartening and mind-boggling why the Canadian governments, as well as non-indigenous individuals, would engage in brutally suppressing Indigenous culture and committing barbarous atrocities. In 2008, a "little bird" tapped Stephen Harper on the shoulder, reminding him of the negative relations existing between the non-indigenous and Indigenous peoples. Lo and behold! Stephen Harper rose up in Parliament and apologized to Indigenous peoples on behalf of the nation. However, upon further consideration, it turned out to be a shallow, empty and superficial apology. When the Truth Reconciliation Commission (TRC) requested release of documentation pertaining to residential schools, Harper's refusal to cooperate led to costly suit and legal proceedings with the Canadian government. What kind of democracy, if any, does former Prime Minister Harper subscribe to? Fortunately, TRC obtained the documentation it requested on the residential schools, but only after a court ruling.

TRC's 2015 document, after seven years of research, was the first major attempt to show how Conservative and Liberal regimes employed residential schools as one instrument—among others—to defame, degrade and destroy Indigenous culture and

---

19   Ibid. p. 27.

20   Ibid. p. 27.

way of life. According to TRC, 150,000 Indigenous children were forcefully taken from their families and placed in the notorious residential schools.[21] According to the testimonials presented to TRC, Indigenous children were victims of many abuses and criminal behaviour. As stated by TRC, "residential schooling was always more than simply an educational program—it was an integral part of a conscious policy of cultural genocide."[22]

It should be underscored that Canadian government and non-indigenous people didn't simply seek to disrupt the lives of Indigenous children; their mission was to destroy and erase Indigenous culture and way of life. From the time of Confederation, the aims of successive governments were to seize Indian lands, move Indigenous peoples onto reserves, dismantle their political and social institutions, enforce the prohibition of the use of their language and cultural ceremonies, and convert them to Christianity.

With respect to Christianity, it should be noted that the higher echelons of the church were part of the Indigenous genocidal process. According to the papal decree, Canada and non-indigenous Europeans in Canada had the right, as did the Spaniards in South America, to conquer and convert Indigenous peoples to Christianity. Moreover, European settlers migrating to Canada held the racist view that they were a superior race and possessed the unequivocal right to civilize "savages" and convert them to a Christian lifestyle.

Non-indigenous people and Canadian governments have much work to do, not only to acknowledge the wrongs that have been committed against the Indigenous peoples, but to take the necessary steps to get at the truth.Speaking bluntly, non-indigenous Canadians need to make use of the much-coveted and

---

21   National Centre for Truth and Reconciliation. "Honouring the Truth, Reconciling for the Future." http://nctr.ca/reports.php

22   Ibid.

extolled scientific method—it entails gathering of facts, necessitates studying the 2015 TRC report, subjecting the facts and report to analysis and logically extrapolating more truthful conclusions.

Careful scrutiny is required to determine why Sir John A. MacDonald and his Conservative regime embarked on such a vicious genocidal journey. A number of analytical scholars, including TRC's report, take the view that economic and corporate interests mounted enormous pressure on the MacDonald government to espouse the genocidal policy with respect to Indigenous peoples.

Pressure on the MacDonald government came from several quarters: railway companies, need for Western settlement, annexation threat from United States, as well as some influence from higher echelons of religious authorities. Echoing the words of TRC: "since confederation, but even more pointedly during the greater part of the 20th century, it became legislative practice to erase indigenous peoples, primarily for economic interests. It would have been (and still would be) fiscally impossible for the crown to fully meet its treaty obligations.[23]

The obvious conclusion is that the MacDonald government, and successive Conservative and Liberal regimes, adhered to the genocidal policies, desecrated authentic Christian principles, degraded Canadian democracy and totally abandoned humanitarian ideals. The most desirable way to conclude this short chapter on the plight of Indigenous peoples in Canada is to note the TRC statement that the residential school system is "difficult to accept as something that could have happened in a country such as Canada, which has long prided itself on being a bastion of democracy, peace and kindness throughout the world".[24]

---

23   *New Trail.* Volume 73.1, Spring 2017. p. 26.

24   National Centre for Truth and Reconciliation. "Honouring the Truth, Reconciling for the Future." p. 1.

CHAPTER 4

Western World in State of Decay

On Sunday, August 14, 2005, Michael Coren wrote an article in the *Edmonton Sun*, entitled: "TERRORISTS ARE RIGHT: THE WEST IS DECADENT." He wrote, "The gap between the rich and poor is greater than it has been for a century, and multi-national corporations tell us what to drink, what to think and what to do. The environment is raped, the planet abused and our dinner portions grow larger."

Michael Coren appears to have displayed great foresight more than a decade ago, pointing to signs of decadence which we are witnessing today in the Western world. We are experiencing a moral dilemma and crisis on a scale that we have never seen before. Perhaps, in a small way, Western decadence can be compared to Roman Empire decadence, best illustrated by Emperor Nero, who played the fiddle while Rome was burning.

Ample evidence is available, indicating that the Western world, under American hegemony, has descended into a culture of decadence and moral quagmire. This is clearly exemplified by sex scandals, extensive and horrific violence, and widening economic and social inequality. Further evidence illustrating the decadent trend of the Western world is its involvement in the Middle Eastern wars. The Western power structures, which include the multi-national corporations, promote the costly Middle Eastern wars, sacrificing the money that's needed to upgrade American and European infrastructure that's in a state of disrepair. Moreover, American and European power structures view the raping of the environment in a cavalier manner, paying little attention to global, environmental and climate change danger, and existential nuclear threat is given even less consideration.

Regarding sexual behaviour, we are witnessing increasing cases of sexual harassment and assault involving people of high status, as exemplified by two American business tycoons, Bill O'Reilly of Fox News and Harvey Weinstein, a Hollywood celebrity. There are many other people of high status, as well as politicians who have transgressed and got involved in sexual misconduct. It's important to underscore that public awareness of sexual harassment is rather low despite the attention ascribed to the #MeToo and Time's Up movements in the United States. Surveys show that North Americans and Europeans underestimate the levels of sexual harassment experienced by women. A more extensive survey was conducted after the #MeToo campaign in 2016, triggered by Hollywood tycoon/producer Harvey Weinstein's alleged sexually-abusive behaviour towards female actors. The survey revealed that men were more reluctant to recognize the extent of sexual harassment, which held back efforts to take action on the issue. Interestingly, in the UK, unions have repeatedly emphasized that low-paid workers were so subjected to harassment and abuse, that it had become entirely normalized and routine.

A similar pattern of violence and sexual harassment is common and tends to be practised in other European nations.

It's critical to grasp the understanding that, over the years, a culture of sexual harassment evolved in the Western world which is present industry-wide today. North American and European industries are primarily organized in the workplace on the top-down command model. Inevitably, such a system creates conditions of sexual vulnerability for workers, in that it's common for a female employee to be working under male supervision and authority. Sexual misconduct may transpire should the authoritative male happen to share the culture of sexual harassment.

It's fair to assert that when sexual drives of males are reinforced by the status of wealth and economic power, by holding an authoritative position, as well as being conditioned by the tradition of male chauvinism, the ugly head of male dominance is likely to surface and lead to sexual harassment and misconduct.

To erode and minimize sexual harassment, societies of necessity need to embark on implementing policies leading to greater social and economic equality. Creating a more egalitarian society will ultimately create the necessary conditions for gender equality, which will set the stage for suppressing, decreasing and possibly eliminating sexual harassment.

Various forms and categories of violence are universal in scope; however, the Western world, the United States in particular, has more than its share of violence. In October 2017, 58 people were killed, and several hundreds were injured, in a mass shooting in Las Vegas. Without going into detailed description, there have been multiple shootings in the United States in recent years—shootings in malls, schools, churches, night clubs, etc.; in fact, violence in the United States is as "common as cherry pie", as expressed by an American social activist. Sadly, violence in the United States is a daily occurrence.

Proportionally, in relation to population, Canada and many nations of Europe also experience their share of violent behaviour. The daily atrocities in the United States have been characterized by President Donald Trump as that of "mentally-deranged" individuals. However, American corporate media is virtually silent and hesitant to offer an explanation on the cause of the wide-spread occurrence of violence in America. Even psychologists are baffled by the individual acts of violence in society, and appear to be unable or reluctant to provide a more definitive answer on the cause of violence.

Some scholars put forth the view that values people are exposed to in society have much to do with their mental affliction and the propensity to commit violent acts. The constant bombardment of commercialism and violence on television, persistent exposure to a confused and disorderly world, existence of growing poverty and the lack of clear purpose in life most likely contribute to so-called "mental derangement". Existence of such conditions propel an individual over the edge and make him commit inexplicable acts of violence.

However, it should be pointed out there are also crimes committed by perfectly sane individuals—people who are materially motivated and engage in criminal activity by robbing grocery stores, financial institutions and other industrial enterprises. Individuals of this category justify their criminal behaviour knowingly by taking a risk for material gain. Being out of work, seeking adventure and rejecting the norms, values and laws of society inevitably drives the individual to choose a path of crime and potential violence.

Notwithstanding, the violence and crimes committed by individuals, the most notorious and hideous crimes, atrocities and violence are perpetrated by gangs and mobsters. Some time ago, mafia-related gangs gained considerable attention; more recently, Mexican gangs led by the notorious El Chapo (now in captivity) are making headline news. Unfortunately, in the Western world, the rationale on gang-related crimes and violence can be traced back to the Hobbesian "human nature" argument (i.e. people by nature are greedy, brutish, egoistic and motivated by personal gain and material aggrandizement). According to this type of thinking, crime and violence by gangs and individuals who are motivated by economic gain are here to stay. However, many scholars and others argue that materially motivated gang violence has much to do with how the economic system is organized. It can be argued that a more equitable distribution of wealth and income, a marked movement towards an "egalitarian" society and its values, would dramatically lower gang crime and violence over time.

As a value judgment, the most despicable, massive and severe forms of violence are those motivated politically and ideologically, as expressed by war. Since World War II, several wars have occurred which require examining; in particular, the Vietnam and Iraqi wars. Both wars were essentially fought by the United States; Britain, France, Germany and other allies played a nominal role in these two wars. In the case of Vietnam, former American Minister of Defence, Ed McNamara, stated in his documentary *The Fog of War* that the United States should have never been involved in the war—that it committed a political and moral blunder. With reference to the Iraqi war, it's been established the war was not about G. W. Bush and the so-called "weapons of mass destruction" supposedly controlled by Saddam Hussein; on the contrary, the war was engineered by the Bush administration based on carefully orchestrated "weapons of mass deception". Facts don't lie; the Kennedy and Johnson administrations didn't provide us with truth on Vietnam, nor did the Bush administration articulate voraciously to the public on the Iraqi war.

Concerning the conflicts in the Middle East, two diametrically-opposed points of view have surfaced and are being argued.

The more popular point of view, which argues in support of American foreign policy, is that the United States and Western powers are victims of the evil activities of radical Islamic terrorism, including Isis. Other terror groups such as the Taliban, Al Qaeda and Al Nostra are conducting activities in conjunction with Isis, although their relationship with Isis is unclear. Another avowed terror group is operating in Africa under the name of Boko Haram. The Trump administration added Hezbollah of Lebanon and North Korea to the terror list, but a new relationship has evolved between Donald Trump and Kim Jong Un of North Korea, with the consequence that North Korea is no longer on the terror list. The United States and North Korea summits held in June 2018 and February 2019 offer some hope on demilitarizing the Korean peninsula. However, close observation and analysis suggests that North Korea will unlikely be inclined to take further concrete steps towards demilitarization as long as the United States maintains its troops in South Korea and keeps its naval presence in the peninsula.

Many people and scholars posit the unpopular view arguing that the United States and its allies fail to take into account and explain the real motivation of Islamic terror groups and Isis. A number of analysts have concluded that the foreign policies of the United States and its allies are based on falsehood and deception. The question they ask is, why is the United States and its allies so deeply preoccupied with the Middle East? Is it because the Western world is motivated in promoting the ideals of freedom and democracy in the Middle East, or is it something else?

It's being argued that the West, under the hegemony of the United States, is waging a war on terror with the aim of exercising domination and control over oil-rich Muslim and Arab territory. An important segment of the Arab and Muslim world subscribe to the view that their struggle in the Middle East is that of "national liberation" and regard Western involvement as imperialism.

It should be pointed out that the Sunni nationality and nation, formerly of Iraq, was destroyed by the second Bush invasion. With the dismemberment of Iraq, Sunni activists adopted a strong belief in Islamic nationalism and formed the core of Isis movement, committed to establishing an Islamic nation state. While Isis has made impressive gains in early stages of its struggle, it was ultimately subdued by the superior strength and air power of the United States, its allies and Russia.

While the Islamic state was virtually eliminated, it would appear that the dream of Sunni people and their Islamic supporters for an Islamic nation state in the Middle East has been placed on hold. Isis activists and their supporters have scattered

throughout the Middle East, Europe and an undetermined number in North America. Time will tell what strategy the remnant
Sunni leadership will adopt; however, destabilization of the
Middle East by the two warring sides, which precipitated a major
refugee crisis, does not bode well for the Middle East, Europe
or North America. According to Donald Trump's announcement on February 5, 2019, Isis has been defeated. Trump argues
that it's time to bring American soldiers home from Syria and
Afghanistan. However, one can pose the question: why have
5,000 American troops been placed in Columbia?

Widening gap between rich and poor

Returning to Michael Coren's article, the "gap between the
rich and poor is greater than it has been for a century" rings
true for many Canadians. It's no mystery why the gap is widening; indisputably, it's the consequence of an economy based on
the profit motive which allows individuals to engage in entre-
preneurial ventures to amass wealth. In examining history, for
roughly a thousand years, the period between the collapse of the
Western Roman Empire in the latter part of the 5th century, and
the emergence of modern Europe in the 15th century, applying
the profit motive and taking advantage of people monetarily was
prohibited and regarded as improper, sinful and usury.

However, with the emergence of mercantilism and embryonic capitalism, banks and a monetary exchange system, organizing a business around the profit motive became proper,
acceptable and legal. Over time, business ventures mushroomed
and the foundation for accumulation of wealth set the stage for
the unfolding of modern capitalism. Since the 1500s, economies in Europe, the United States and Canada have evolved and
matured, giving rise to the formation of financial oligopolies,
monopolies and oligarchies. Many scholars have advanced the
view that uncontrolled concentration of wealth at the top and
the rise of plutocracies undermine the basic core of democratic
society. There is ample evidence showing that the gap between

the few at the top and the majority at the bottom continues to widen in the West.

There is a growing consensus among many Canadians that the widening gap between rich and poor is an inherent feature of the economy. It is argued that under the profit motive, the market economy inevitably paves the way for corporations to amass massive fortunes. This literally means workers and their families have less purchasing power to buy the abundance of goods available in the market place. The result is that the economy becomes confronted by an economic contradiction or paradox when so much capital or money is concentrated at the top of the pyramid, inevitably resulting in diminution of buying power among people at the bottom. A popular adage provides clarity to the contradiction by saying "you can't eat the cake and have it too."

However, despite the economic dilemma, the Canadian economy continues to function in an undulating fashion. To compensate for lack of purchasing power, credit cards, mortgages and banking systems play a significant role in increasing the money supply to assist the domestic market. Introduction of these measures increases economic activity and helps to alleviate the economic contradiction; but at the same time, it places many Canadians in worrisome and uncomfortable debt. Accumulation of surplus commodities reflects the serious nature of the dilemma faced by the economy and compels corporations to search for markets outside the country. Undoubtedly, Prime Minister Trudeau's visitation to China in December 2017, although relations are somewhat complicated, is precisely related to the issue of trade, anticipating new markets to be negotiated for the disposal of surplus Canadian commodities.

Turning to Michael Coren again, his statement that "multinational corporations tell us what to drink, what to think and what to do" requires some attention.Multi-national corporations have international connections and are intertwined with the Canadian composite, invisible and ghost-like power struc-

ture.[25] The most influential element of the power structure is
the corporate elite, consisting of the Canadian Council of Chief
Executives, with a large CEO corporate membership, representing huge assets and wealth. There is strong evidence suggesting
that multi-national corporations exercise substantive influence
on neoliberalism, which is the foundation of Canadian ideological thinking.

Multi-national corporations rely on the media to provide
effective advertising, encouraging consumers to buy the commodities being produced. Using their boundless resources,
corporate media saturates commercial TV ads in an attempt to
influence public thinking on consumption. Considerable evidence available suggests a close correlation between commercial advertising and public consumption habits.

There is widespread concern among many people that consumerism motivated by the profit motive has run amuck. It
remains to be seen whether rational behaviour and modest consumption will reverse the current trend of excessive consumerism. People argue that reversing the trend of consumption is an
uphill battle in that decisions on the issue of consumerism is
exclusively in the hands of multi-national corporations.

Should the issue of "consumerism" arise in Canadian
Parliament, it's more likely the Canadian power structure would
kick in, requesting Prime Minister Trudeau quash the debate
and kill the issue. A recent example of an issue demonstrating the influence of the Canadian power structure is the sale of
armaments to Saudi Arabia. When the armaments agreement
came before Parliament for approval, Prime Minister Trudeau
signed the agreement, providing minimal debate on the issue.
Sadly, the armaments sale put Trudeau and Canadians in a
moral quagmire, since the armaments are now being used by

---

25   See Footnote 13 for explanation.

the Saudi regime to kill innocent people, women and children in Yemen.

It is fitting and proper to conclude the chapter by referring to Michael Coren's statement again, where he says "the environment is raped, the planet abused." Indeed, he hit the nail on the head; the world and humanity is confronted with the worst pollution, greenhouse gas emissions, environmental degradation and nuclear armaments build-up on a scale that we've never seen before. In keeping with Michael Coren's thinking, climate change compounded by environmental devastation and the suicidal nuclear arms race, constitute the two most serious existential threats facing the planet.

Environmentalists have expressed real concern about climate change, environmental degradation and the continuing increase in greenhouse emissions. There is a consensus that transportation and burning coal are the leading and fastest-growing contributors to greenhouse gas emissions. Forests and vegetation have difficultly absorbing excess gas emissions; the leaves and needles are the most valuable solar collectors. Wood is the most abundant and renewable source of energy on the planet and should be declared a sacred element in society. Wood has been used from time immemorial and societies have taken it for granted.

It needs to be highlighted that global pollution is an integral part of climate change. Pollution can cause breaches in the ozone layer, which can bring toxins to rivers, air and soil, which literally means devastation of the environment. The impacts of global pollution are best exemplified by the disruption of the Great Barrier Reef and the rapid melting of Arctic ice.

In examining the second existential threat, namely, the possibility of nuclear war resulting in nuclear winter and holocaust, the profound feelings and belief of humanity is that such a catastrophic occurrence cannot and will not take place. However, common sense and logic tells us that such noble thinking must be grounded in reality. How can people reconcile their beliefs when two atomic bombs were detonated in 1945 on Hiroshima and Nagasaki?

Sorrowfully and unhappily, world disarmament is not being discussed by world leaders, and the issue has descended to low on the priority list. It's troublesome to accept the premise that the technology of building a crude nuclear weapon is currently within the reach of motivated, educated and well-financed militants. One can project many scenarios where a nuclear war can erupt; it can happen by a computer glitch, miscalculation by major powers or out of uncontrollable regional conflict.

According to William J. Perry, "today the danger of some sort of a nuclear catastrophe is greater than it was during the cold war."[26]

It's encouraging that William Perry established the William Perry project, with the aim of promoting an understanding of the horrific danger of nuclear war. California governor Jerry Brown remarked that he knows of no person other than William Perry who has a better grasp of the science and politics of nuclear weaponry.

People who support peace and not war have a great challenge before them to build a movement that can lay the basis for disarmament and a nuclear-free world. The great challenge in effort to build a viable peace movement is overcoming the lack of awareness among the public; the millennial generation in particular have been socially conditioned into believing that the issue of nuclear war has been resolved. The corporate media does not promote world peace; it promotes the armaments industry, which accumulates vast sums of money generated by current wars.

What is required at this historic junction is cessation of missile testing, followed by an agreement for total disarmament by

---

26   Perry, William J. Speech at the Washington National Cathedral. November 30, 2017.

all nations and reinforced by a comprehensive verification system.

The Dalai Lama articulated some time ago that Hiroshima and Nagasaki should be a reminder to all of us about the destructive nature of war and nuclear weapons. During his visitation to Londonderry on September 11, 2017, he said "we must seriously make efforts, step by step, for a nuclear-free world."[27]

After examining the Western world in decay, we can arrive at the conclusion that many people are reluctant to understand the critical issues, especially the real dangers posed by the two existential threats—climate change (environmental degradation) and nuclear war.

27   Dalai Lama. Speech at Londonderry. September 11, 2017.

CHAPTER 5

Invisible Canadian Political Power Structure

Noam Chomsky published a book entitled *Who Rules the World*. This could also extend to: Who rules Canada? Conventional wisdom tells us, although Canada is regarded as a constitutional monarchy, national decision-making is a fundamental right accorded to elected representatives of Canadian Parliament. The leader of the political party that wins the majority of seats becomes the prime minister, forms a cabinet and governs the nation according to established democratic practice and rule of law.

However, upon closer scrutiny of Canadian democracy, there is reason to believe that a clandestine power structure plays an important role in the decision-making process, especially when critical issues are involved. The Canadian power structure works secretly behind the scenes and is activated for action when the need arises. Multiple names have been ascribed to the term power structure: establishment, "men at the top", capitalist class, ruling class, power elite, military-industrial complex, deep state, etc. Before we delve into the process of how decisions are made in Canadian society, it's necessary and advisable to examine a few notable authors on the subject of power structures.

The most researched and documented work on the issue where real power resides is that of C. Wright Mills' *The Power*

Elite.[28] However, important recognition must also be given to Dwight D. Eisenhower, who, in his farewell speech, warned American people about the danger and threat posed by the military-industrial complex.[29]

On the basis of his extensive research work, C. Wright Mills concluded that intertwined and interconnected interests of three basic groups—military, economics and politics—manipulate the public in secret with respect to critical issues. Of the three sectors of power, according to Mills, the most influential in deciding crucial policy matters is in the hands of the corporate interests. However, the power elite cannot be understood as being the sole reflection of only the economic elites; rather, it is the outcome of an identifiable alliance of economic, political and military forces.

Eisenhower warned American people of the dangers they face; he stated the following: "In the councils of government, we must guard against the acquisition of unwarranted influence, whether sought or unsought, by the military-industrial complex. The potential for the disastrous rise of misplaced power exists and will persist."[30]

He warned the American people that the subtle combination of two elements—military and industry—may seriously endanger American civil liberties and the democratic process. Even more so, Eisenhower stressed the importance of being cognizant, aware and keeping a watchful eye on activities of the military-industrial complex. It's absolutely necessary and critical at this historic juncture to speak up and warn humanity about the danger posed by the American military-industrial complex.

Eisenhower's most noble remark was that "disarmament, with mutual trust, honour and confidence, is a continuing pro-

---

28   Mills, C. Wright. *The Power Elite*. Oxford University Press, 1956.

29   Eisenhower, Dwight D. Farewell Speech, 1961.

30   Ibid.

cess. Together, we must learn how to compose differences, not with arms, but with intellect and decent purpose."[31] Undoubtedly, he expressed concern about the gravest threat humanity is facing today—the threat of a nuclear holocaust.

By reaching out not-too-far on a limb, it is fair to say that Canadians share the values expressed by Eisenhower, but it also evokes questions: How are key decisions made in Canada? Are Canadians also victims of a clandestine power structure? Considerable evidence available reveals the harsh reality that Canada has been a victim of key issues being decided by the power structure and not the federal government.

There are multiple definitions of power structure, but the consensus seems to be that power structures consist of non-governmental people from industry, banks and other financial institutions who have access to all information and govern in secrecy. A more comprehensive definition can be expressed in the following way: Canadian power structure is a composite, invisible and ghost-like structure consisting of a number of identifiable elements.[32] As in the case of other power structures, the Canadian power structure adheres to a strategy which best serves the interests of the corporate elite. The political power structure is activated when policies debated in the House of Commons seriously threaten interests of banks, military industry or big corporations.

Three notable examples illustrating the influence the Canadian power structure exerts on policy decision-making

---

31   Ibid.

32   Composite, invisible and ghost-like power structure consists principally of seven institutions; they are all intertwined, and each has a distinctive role to play. The most powerful element is the corporate sector, which is reinforced by other elements such as the banks, military, police, secret service, corporate media and the higher echelons of religion. All the institutions operate according to the command top-down model.

are (1) the case of the NAFTA Agreement (1992), (2) the sale of arms to Saudi Arabia in 2017 and (3) SNC-Lavalin scandal in 2019. In the case of NAFTA, Mulroney caved in to the composite and invisible power structure by approving the agreement with minimal debate in Parliament. Similarly, in the matter of armaments sold to Saudi Arabia, after receiving a phone call from the power structure, Prime Minister Trudeau signed former Prime Minister Harper's arms agreement with little time for questioning in Parliament. With respect to SNC-Lavalin scandal, evidence seems to suggest that Prime Minister Trudeau again succumbed to corporate power; subsequently, he interfered and exerted sustained pressure on the Auditor General, giving her no choice but resignation.

Shortly after Confederation and the birth of the Dominion of Canada, Sir John A. MacDonald and his Conservative government implemented legislation for governing Indigenous peoples of Canada. It's rather puzzling and strange why the MacDonald government, officially a proponent of democracy and Christianity, would enact legislation aimed at the degradation and destruction of Indigenous peoples and their culture. Openly and knowingly, it was stated in Parliament by Sir John A. MacDonald that Indigenous peoples were "savages".[33] For more than a century, Indigenous peoples were victims of the barbarous and despicable Conservative and Liberal government policies.

Interestingly, with the Confederation of Canada in 1867, there was also the genesis of a nascent, embryonic Canadian power structure. This newly-formed power structure, from its inception, exercised enormous influence on the MacDonald government, as well as on successive Conservative and Liberal regimes.

---

33   *New Trail*. Volume 73.1, Spring 2017. p. 27.

Formation of the racist and notorious residential schools and brutal suppression of Metis struggle for self-government and democracy are a reflection of the influence that was exercised by the evolving Canadian power structure. As recently as 2013, when the Truth Reconciliation Commission (TRC) asked the Harper government for pertinent Indigenous documents, it was necessary to launch legal proceedings.[34]

Clearly, the entrenched Canadian power structure shows a history of influencing governmental policies on critical issues. On many occasions, Conservative and Liberal regimes danced to the tune provided by the Canadian power structure.[35] Recently, Trans-Pacific Partnership (TPP) has been getting considerable publicity. According to Joseph Stiglitz, world-renowned Nobel Prize Economist, TPP is the worst trade deal ever negotiated. With power structures operating behind the scenes, a provision has been inserted into TPP which allows multi-national corporations to sue governments should their economic interests surface as a critical issue. Inserting such a clause into the trade agreement is outrageous and preposterous, but power structures claim to know what's best for society.

Trying to unravel the enigmatical relationships that exist between Canada and the United States is of considerable interest and a great challenge. Recent NAFTA negotiations between the two nations appear to indicate that the United States and its military-industrial complex have the upper hand, as revealed by the imposition of tariffs on Canadian aluminum and steel products.When it comes to the Canadian economy, it's not surprising that Canada developed a distorted economy. Canada established

---

34   Ibid.

35   Post-Confederation, CPR Railway and the private banks, the most important elements of the Canadian power structure, exerted a profound impact on the MacDonald government. The railway companies laid the basis for settling the West with total disregard for Indigenous peoples.

a viable primary and tertiary industry but a rather weak and feeble secondary industry. As a result, Canadians are now paying a heavy price for not developing a balanced economy. Since the end of World War II, Canadian governments have been negligent and fail to keep a sharp eye on American intrusion into the Canadian economy. An unbalanced Canadian economy, lacking a vibrant secondary industry, has serious implications for Canada with respect to job creation and employment.

There is evidence indicating that the Canadian political power structure is enmeshed and closely interwoven with and submissive to the American military-industrial complex. When conflictual issues arise as illustrated by NAFTA negotiations, the Canadian power structure and government tends to succumb to the United States and its power structure. It seems evident that Canadian decision-makers have a close but a subservient relationship with the United States. The American government and its power structure negotiate from a position of strength when it comes to serious trade matters; consequently, Canadian democracy and Canadian interests are sacrificed.[36]

Clearly, American authorities have virtually reduced Canada's secondary industry to insignificance and have thwarted development of a balanced economy. Whether Canadians will rise to the occasion and exert sufficient pressure on the Canadian government to adopt a realistic strategy to effect resuscitation of secondary industry remains to be seen.

In the matter of Canadian foreign policy, scrutiny suggests that Canada tends to reflect American foreign policy. Canada is closely linked to the United States and toes the American foreign policy line. The fact that Canada's economy is so closely integrated with the American economy makes it extremely dif-

---

36   Democracy is derived from the Greek word "demos", meaning "people", and "kratos", meaning "rule". In the Canadian context, it means that a majority make decisions on key issues.

ficult, if not impossible under present circumstances, to pursue
an independent Canadian foreign policy.

CHAPTER 6

Mystery Underlying the Canadian Banking System

The importance of studying banking

It's questionable how much Canadians really know how banks operate. Most Canadians simply look at the bank as a place to deposit surplus cash, receive some interest on their money and apply for a loan if they have a project in mind. But question—How did banks come into being? What is role of the Bank of Canada (BOC)? Who regulates the money supply in Canada? How did the five major banks accumulate so much capital? Is it true with a million-dollar bank deposit, banks can lend out many times that amount and charge interest on those loans?

A small survey of the questions asked tells us that many Canadians have difficulty in responding to the banking process, as it is shrouded in secrecy and confusion. It's interesting to note that many bank managers appear to be in the dark with respect to how their own banks operate.

A number of economists and scholars posit the view that the Canadian political power structure and government prefers that Canadians know as little as possible on the operation of Canadian banking. The corporate media, one of the tentacles of the power structure, seldom talks about the banking system and intentionally avoids informing the public about the operation of banking. Canadian banks report their quarterly income every so often but do not clearly state how they arrived at that income. If one is to understand how private chartered banks operate, it is crucial to examine the origin and evolution of the banking system.

As early as 1157, the Bank of Venice was established by the Medici family, and they introduced the double entry bookkeeping system, letters of credit and holding companies. However, it wasn't until mid-17th century (1640), with the emergence of a growing merchant class, that modern banking began with the English goldsmiths.[37] Subsequently, modern banks were established in India, Germany and other European centres. Historically, there is an abundance of evidence which clearly shows it was the merchant bankers who first established and evolved a system of banking. Initially, trading was in commodities and not in money; however, it wasn't long before trade in commodities was to be replaced by an exchange and trade with money.

In the development of banking, a big leap occurred when goldsmiths became involved in banking. As the mercantile economy developed, the number of merchants grew in number, and a major problem surfaced for the merchants—how were they going to secure accumulated gold bullion, money and ornaments? In response to the problem, merchants sought out honest individuals, a "goldsmith", to protect gold, jewellery and other valuables.

For taking on the responsibility of safekeeping, goldsmiths established a policy of issuing a receipt, which is equivalent to a cheque, as evidence of receiving the valuables. Since the gold and silver coins had no markings of the owner, the goldsmith soon discovered and grasped an opportunity; he engaged in

---

37   Smriti Chand. "Banking: The Evolution, Origin and Growth of Banking."
http://www.yourarticlelibrary.com/banking/banking-the-evolution-origin-and-growth-of-banking/10998

a process of lending the valuables to customers. Holder of the receipt was secure in that he would receive an equal amount of money which he had deposited with the goldsmith on demand.

It wasn't long before the goldsmith made a further discovery—close observation showed him that, over a period of time, withdrawals of valuables were always much less than the deposits placed with him. For looking after the valuables, the goldsmith began charging a fee, which came to be known as interest. To protect himself, the goldsmith kept some money as reserve.

As the economy developed, the goldsmiths/money-lenders became bankers. With a spiralling merchant and market economy, with a great increase in wealth and commerce in Europe, private banks mushroomed rapidly and became an accepted institution under embryonic capitalism.

The Canadian system of banking was inherited from the colonial British Empire. After the Seven Years' War (1756-1763) between Britain and France, New France became a colony of Britain. Significant growth of population in the territories under British control led to the Confederation of Canada in 1867—a union of four provinces known as the Dominion of Canada. By Confederation, the banking system in a Canada was in full swing. Private banks played a pivotal role in financing railway companies, which helped in promoting settlement of Western Canada. Over the past 150 years, Canada has evolved five major banks, with Royal Bank displaying the most assets. There is also the Bank of Canada (BOC); however, the relationship between it and the five major banks is enigmatical, obscure and unclear.

How does the Canadian banking system work?

Let us assume that the Prime Minister of Canada and the government are one billion dollars short in their budget (they need an additional one billion dollars). How does the government get the one billion dollars? According to an established practice, the government makes a request and authorizes the Treasury Board to print one billion dollars in Canadian bonds.

After being printed, the Treasury Board delivers the bonds to government—bonds owned by the Bank of Canada (BOC). The Bank of Canada, in possession of the bonds, sells the bonds to private chartered bank. Here is the kicker—the chartered bank pays for bonds by creating a bank deposit on behalf of the federal government. It's simply amazing! The chartered bank created one billion dollars that didn't exist before—it was created out of thin air. The startling conclusion is that the chartered bank now owns one billion dollars' worth of Canadian government bonds, while the Canadian government is in debt to a tune of one billion dollars. And the most disturbing conclusion of the process is that the Canadian tax payers are obliged to pay interest on these bonds to the private chartered bank. It's worth noting that the cost of creating one billion dollars costs the chartered bank virtually nothing, except for the cost of cancelling out government cheques as it writes them against the deposit.

There is more to the story of banking—under the "fractional reserve system," chartered banks can take the government bond which they have bought, create a deposit and use it as a reserve to create more bank deposits.

Under the current fractional reserve system, new money only goes into circulation when someone takes a loan from the bank. The more money people borrow from a bank, which increases the money supply, the more buoyant the economy becomes. The reverse takes place when people pay back their loans; money supply shrinks rapidly and becomes scarce, propelling the economy into a slump.

However, as mentioned earlier, when banks create new money via the fractional reserve system, national debt is also created—if an individual is approved for a mortgage loan, the money provided is only a digital entry in the bank account—the money given was created out of thin air. The money did not come from the reserves or deposits. Isn't that a clever way of making money and accumulating capital?

Nowadays, Canadian banks, as do most modern banks, operating under the fractional reserve system are allowed to keep only a small fraction of their reserves; the rest of the reserves are utilized for lending purposes. Banks operate under the assumption that not all people will withdraw their funds from the bank, thus, bank stability will be maintained.

In recent years, it wasn't smooth sailing for Canadian banks, as reported by the corporate media. During the 2007-2008 economic slump and US sub-prime crisis, the US housing bubble popped, while the Canadian housing bubble continued to develop, creating further mal-investments promoted by the low interest environment. Have Canadians learned anything from the 2008-2009 sub-prime crisis?

Many Canadians are concerned that, as the housing bobble continues to grow, there appears to be minimal discussion on the impending crisis, which can easily implode. Let us look at some facts. As of October 2008, an individual could qualify for a mortgage loan at 5% down payment, and some banks offer 5% cash back, which ultimately means that an individual can buy a house with no money down.

In effort to avoid the housing disaster experienced by the United States, US Fed and Bank of Canada (BOC) arranged short-term collateralized loans to Canadian banks and Canadian Mortgage Housing Corporation (CMHC)—owned by the Canadian federal government. The two financial institutions bought $69 billion worth of mortgages from Canadian chartered banks. The high point of support for Canadian banks was attained in 2009, amounting to a sum of $114 billion, which is equivalent to 7% of the total Canadian economy.[38]

A troublesome scenario is that a slump could precipitate a deflationary situation, causing fallen prices in properties and commodities; this would likely continue until the market econ-

---

38 "Canada's Banking System Exposed." Mises Canada, 2015. p. 4.

omy attained equilibrium. To preclude a downward economic trend on a global basis, central banks are engaging in Keynesian economics to create stimulus programs (priming the pump) in effort to maintain an inflationary period to avoid selfimploding.

In effort to secure greater stability, Canadian banks have offloaded their mortgages to CMHC, which now holds $300 billion worth of Canadian mortgages, besides insuring an additional $600 billion worth of mortgages.[39] It is worrisome and frightening that in the event of a serious downturn and default, Canadian tax payers would be obliged to honour the losses. It should be mentioned that too many Canadians have fallen for the superficial understanding that their deposit in the bank is safeguarded and that 100% of their money could be withdrawn at any time; that's fairytale thinking and is fallacious. Moreover, it should be revealed that Canadian banks have virtually no gold reserves to speak of, unlike many other nations.

For the time being, Canada's monetary situation appears to be stable; however, the future remains in doubt.

A number of economists and scholars have come up with different ideas how a stable monetary system can be established. John Maynard Keynes, a notable authority on monetary systems, said that governments should borrow large sums of money and apply it to extensive public works projects. In his view, by priming the economy, also known as quantitative easing (i.e. by increasing the money supply and expanding the circulation of money), a vibrant economy could be maintained and economic slumps could be avoided.[40] Democratic capitalistic countries have adopted much of Keynesian theory on monetary policy, but economic indicators seem to suggest that the issues of economic slumps and unemployment remain unresolved.

---

39   Ibid. p. 10.

40   Keynes, John Maynard. *The General Theory of Employment, Interest and Money*. Palgrave Macmillan, 1936.

Another economist, Irving Fisher, wrote a book around the same time as Keynes, but Fisher advocated a 100% reserve system, meaning that the government should create the necessary money supply rather than borrow it from private chartered banks.[41]

The positive aspect of a 100% reserve monetary system is that tax payers aren't obliged to pay interest charges to chartered banks for the loans arranged by the government. By this monetary model, the Government of Canada could avoid going into debt.

Interestingly, in 2015, Iceland introduced a monetary system similar to the model suggested by Fisher much earlier. By virtue of the fact that Iceland is a sovereign state with an independent currency, it exercised its freedom and power to reform its monetary system. The government of Iceland rejected and parted with the fractional reserve system to implement a better monetary model, which is favoured by the majority of Icelanders.

In Iceland, as in the other capitalistic market economies, the central bank controls the creation of banknotes and coins, but not the creation of all money. Iceland is contemplating a revolutionary monetary model, denying chartered banks the power to create money and then selling it to the central bank. The proposal was largely engineered and written by a lawmaker of the ruling Centrist Progressive Party, Frosty Sigurjonsson, entitled "Monetary Reform – A better monetary system for Iceland."[42] Under the sovereign monetary model the central bank would become the only creator of money. However, the power of creating money would be kept separate from the power making decisions how the new money is to be spent.

---

41   Fisher, Irving. *100% Money and the Public Debt.*

42   https://www.stjornarradid.is/media/forsaetisraduneyti-media/media/skyrslur/monetary-reform.pdf. p. 10.

In Iceland's sovereign monetary model, all new money which is created by the central bank is either added to governmental finances and spent in the real economy, or it is lent out to chartered banks and other firms that will lend to businesses in the real economy. The positive side of the money created by the central bank is that it would lower public and private debt levels as well as inflation. Banks would continue to manage accounts and serve as intermediaries between savers and lenders.

Other nations are keeping a close eye on the monetary system being introduced in Iceland. The United States, in particular, a major world power, also appears to have problems in its monetary system. The Federal Reserve System and the Treasury Board bailed out the largest financial institutions in the United States, because they were considered too big to fail. Bernie Sanders argues that Wall Street needs to be placed under control. The starting point is to reform the Federal Reserve System so that it keeps close watch on financial institutions as well as the monetary policy in effort to maintain price stability and full employment.

With respect to American banking system, Bernie Sanders has this to say: "To ensure the safety and soundness of our banking system, we need to fundamentally restructure the Fed's governance system to eliminate conflicts of interest. Board members should be nominated by the president and chosen by the Senate. Banking industry executives must no longer be allowed to serve on the Fed's boards and to handpick its members and staff. Board positions should instead include representatives from all walks of life—including labor, consumers, homeowners, urban residents, farmers and small businesses."[43]

---

43   Sanders, Bernie. "To Reign in Wall Street, Fix the Fed." *The New York Times*. https://www.nytimes.com/2015/12/23/opinion/bernie-sanders-to-rein-in-wall-street-fix-the-fed.html

Bernie Sanders makes a further observation when he says that commercial banks should be prohibited from gambling with bank deposits of American people. Undoubtedly, if the United States would implement the monetary model suggested by Bernie Sanders, it would be on much better financial footing. At the moment, as Bernie Sanders puts it, "the Federal Reserve doesn't regulate Wall Street; Wall Street regulates the Fed."[44]

American politics are highly volatile; the outcome of the 2020 presidential election will largely determine if any of the monetary reforms suggested by Bernie Sanders will be considered. Canadians have the option of studying the monetary model chosen by Iceland, or they can look south of the 49th parallel and probe American proposals. By examining the two monetary systems, and by no means excluding others, Canadians may be able to develop a monetary model appropriate for Canada.

It's important that Canadians exert pressure on politicians and governments to examine how the Canadian monetary system is functioning. Canada needs to avoid a repetition of the 2008-2009 economic slump, which entailed the bailout of banking institutions. They certainly need not tolerate a repeat situation, as it happened during the last economic meltdown, involving bailouts where CEOs of the five major Canadian banks were among the highest paid functionaries. For example, Edmund Clark of TD Bank received a compensation package which escalated from $11.1 million in 2008 to $15.2 in 2009.[45] Why was there a need for Canadian banks to be bailed out? Where was the Canadian Prime Minister or Governor of the Bank of Canada (BOC) when the financial packages were being set for CEOs of the respective banks?

It is difficult to end this chapter on a positive note amid mostly bleak economic news. For example, the Edmonton

---

44   Ibid.

45   "Canada's Banking System Exposed." Mises Canada, 2015. p. 5.

Journal reported in March 2019 that Stephen Poloz, governor of the BOC, left the benchmark interest rate unchanged at 1.75%, and said the path to higher borrowing costs was "uncertain."[46] Clearly, it's not just money supply and uncertainty of interest rates that poses serious economic problems; the desperate quest for domestic and foreign markets are an ongoing problem for the Canadian market economy. Historically low interest rates keep the economy from imploding—let's share the hope of Deputy Governor of the BOC, Lynn Patterson, that "spring will bring positive surprise." However, the Keynesian monetary model, the basis of the Canadian economy, involving interchange between "increasing the money supply during a slowdown and contracting the money supply at times of hyper-economic activity is in serious doubt."

---

46   The Edmonton Journal. Section D. March 8, 2019.

CHAPTER 7

The Barbarity and Inhumanity of War

Ordinary people brought up in a cooperative and peaceful environment and not exposed daily to the barrage of ultra-nationalism, fear-mongering and hate, will tend to uphold progressive and humanistic values. However, one can easily slip into a state of depravity and fall victim to the hysteria of war propaganda. Entrenched power structures utilize the corporate media to inculcate aggressive and warlike values into public thinking. As Albert Einstein put it: "In two weeks the sheep-like masses can be worked up by the newspapers into such a state of excited fury that the men are prepared to put on uniform and kill and be killed, for the sake of the worthless aims of a few interested parties."[47]

In the epoch since World War II, the corporate media has been making maximum use of a powerful tool, television, to propagandize aggressive behaviour. During the Cold War period, we were told to beware a "Red" crouched behind every tree; now we are warned there may be a terrorist behind those trees. While the daily bombardment of terrorism is undoubtedly having an impact on the public, a good section of citizenry is trying to understand the different categories of terrorism (i.e. all ter-

---

47   Einstein, Albert. *The World As I See It*. Citadel Press Books, 1956. p. 12.

rorist groups should not be lumped into the same basket; e.g. Mau Mau terrorist Jomo Kenyatta became president of Kenya). Some terrorist groups see themselves as being part of a national liberation movement.

On the nature of war, Albert Einstein says: "War seems to me a mean, contemptible thing: I would rather be hacked in pieces than take part in such an abominable business. And yet so high, in spite of everything, is my opinion of the human race that believe this bogey would have disappeared long ago, had the sound sense of the nations not been systematically corrupted by commercial and political interests acting through the schools and the Press."[48]

Power structures in the Western world, in particular Europe and America, under the sway of neoliberalism, argue and try to convince the public that the main danger facing the West is threats from Russia. However, some scholars and many individuals take a different view, a position extrapolated from Einstein. In his letter to Sigmund Freud on July 30, 1932, with reference to who is instrumental in promoting war, Einstein says: "The craving for power which characterizes the governing class in every nation is hostile to any limitation of the national sovereignty. This political power hunger is wont to batten on the activities of another group, whose aspirations are on purely mercenary, economic lines. I have specially in mind that small but determined group, active in every nation, composed of individuals who, indifferent to social considerations and restraints, regard warfare, the manufacture and sale of arms, simply as an occasion to advance their personal interests and enlarge their personal authoritys."[49]

---

48   Ibid. p. 6-7.

49   See exchange of letters between Albert Einstein and Sigmund Freud. "Why War?" July 30, 1932.

It's proper and advisable to apply Einstein's thesis for an explanation of World War I. For one reason or another, when Grade 12 students are asked "What led to World War I?" students seem to provide the symptoms as being the real cause of World War I. They argue that such factors as secret diplomacy, build-up of armaments, population pressure and economic rivalry collectively caused World War I. When presented with the challenge of demonstrating how the suggested factors caused World War I, attention is quickly diverted to a different issue—human nature. Unfortunately, introducing human nature as the ultimate cause of the war is an escape tactic to avoid confronting the real cause. The poverty of the "symptoms and human nature approach", which is widely propagandized in society, is that it ignores Einstein's thesis and role of power structures. The real decision-makers are the people behind the scenes who made the critical decisions on World War I.

Applying Einstein's thesis, how do we explain occurrence of World War I?

Taking a historical approach, on the eve of the 20th century (1900), three major powers—Great Britain, France and Russia—each colonized, subdivided and controlled huge chunks of world territory, leaving no territory for other nations with ambition. Britain exercised control over vast territory and a massive empire, which justifiably earned it the title of Pac Britannica. France held extensive colonial possessions in Africa and Asia, while the Russian Tsar ruled Russia and all the Slavic people.

The three nations with entrenched power structures, known as Triple Entente, shared a common denominator. Excepting South and Central America, they colonized, subdivided and exercised control over the world. There was virtually no significant territory to colonize should other nations emerge with the desire to build empires.

Much to the surprise and concern of the Triple Entente, their empires were destined to be challenged by the historical emergence of two modern nation states—Italy and Germany. Both nation states made their formal appearance on the European scene in 1870, at about the same time.[50] Austria-Hungary shared some common interests with the two new states.

The two nation states, Italy and Germany, in conjunction with Austria-Hungary, formed a Triple Alliance in direct opposition to the Triple Entente. While there were rivalries and disagreements within the Triple Alliance, the fundamental contradiction was between the two alliances.

By 1914, the two alliances divided into armed camps, were militarized to the hilt and prepared for a major confrontation. The power structures of the two alliances were involved in serious rivalries and disagreements (i.e. Germany and France clashed over Alsace-Lorraine, Russia and Austria over the Balkans and Britain and Germany sparred over their navies and economic power).

Examining the Triple Entente, it's interesting to note, while Britain professed Christianity and displayed parliamentary democracy, that didn't deter it from engaging in imperialistic policies and building a colonial empire. Similarly, France and Russia both propagated Christianity; France claimed to be democratic while Russia was autocratic, but both engaged in empire building.

Interestingly, the Triple Alliance members were all designated constitutional monarchies. Austria-Hungary was involved in rivalry with Russia over the Balkans and had some territorial disputes with Italy, and Italy had ongoing disputes with France in North Africa. German principalities were unified into modern Germany under Bismarck's leadership. World War I was finally triggered with the assassination of Archduke Franz Ferdinand

---

50   History of emergence of the two modern nation states is a topic of study in itself. Suffice to say, nationalism in Italy was guided by three individuals— Cavour, Mazzini and Garibaldi. In Germany, Bismarck had the honour of guiding the German principalities to form a modern nation state.

at Sarajevo. However, the origin and cause of World War I can be traced to the power structures of the two alliances.[51] The power structures of the Triple Entente were not the least interested in sharing their colonies with Triple Alliance members. Since the negotiations didn't make any headway, the power structures of Italy, Austria-Hungary and Germany were determined to dismantle the empires of the Triple Entente. The diametrically-opposed power structures of the two alliances precipitated and caused World War I.

Albert Einstein puts it in his terms how a minority orchestrates a war: "the minority, the ruling class at present, has the schools and press, usually the church as well, under its thumb. This enables it to organize and sway the emotions of the masses, and make its tool of them."[52]

World War I lasted for four years (1914-1918). Russia was in the midst of revolution and ceased hostilities with Germany, experiencing great territorial losses when it signed a treaty with Germany. Lloyd George of Britain, Clemenceau of France and Woodrow Wilson of the United States arranged the Treaty of Versailles, imposing harsh territorial, military and economic conditions on subdued Germany. Of all the treaty provisions, the most contentious issue of the treaty was the "war guilt" clause that was imposed on Germany (i.e. World War I, according to the three architects of the treaty, was caused by Germany).

The question that arises is: What evidence and logic did the three leaders rely on to make their decision?Unfortunately, none of the three distinguished leaders took the time to make an objective analysis on the origin and fundamental cause of World

---

51   Use of the term "power structure" is in keeping with Einstein's reference to his designation of minority which is the ruling class (business tycoons) and has the schools, press, church, military, secret service and police under its control.

52   See exchange of letters between Albert Einstein and Sigmund Freud. "Why War?" July 30, 1932.

War I. The reason is obvious—the three leaders had their minds made up in advance who caused the war. Germany was defeated, forced to surrender and, being the enemy it was blamed for the cause of World War I.

Following World War I, Europe entered a period of economic rejuvenation and reconstruction. Germany suffered more than other nations in Europe due to the heavy reparations imposed on it by the Treaty of Versailles. Economic and social conditions were exacerbated by the passage of the controversial Harley-Smoot Tariff in 1930, aimed to protect domestic industries from foreign imports. By safeguarding their domestic markets and adhering to protectionist policies, the economies of North America and European nations were rapidly plummeting into an economic slump and depression.

Deterioration of economic and social conditions became a fertile ground for the emergence of new and different political power structures, which came under the designation of "fascist ideology". By 1930, three fascist nations, constituting the Axis Powers, appeared on the political scene, led by Mussolini of Italy, Hitler of Germany and Hirohito of Japan.

The mission and aim of the Axis power structures was to carve up world territory according to their imperial preferences. The Japanese fascist power structure was bent on defeating China and exercising territorial control over Southeast Asia. Fascist Italy was aspiring to enhance its empire by establishing a greater foothold in Africa. Thirdly, Hitler and Nazi Germany had taken control of most of Europe with minimal military engagement and casualties. Hitler's avowed aim was to build a Third Reich, based on the Aryan race, which was to last 1,000 years; luckily for humanity, Hitler's dream of a Third Reich lasted only 10 years.

Hence, unlike World War I, which required considerable research and analysis to determine the cause of the war, World War II takes minimal effort to determine the origin and cause of the war. Clearly, three fascist power structures initiated and

plunged the globe into World War II. The big Allied powers—
Great Britain, the United Kingdom, the United States, France
and the Soviet Union (USSR)—were confronted by the Axis
Powers.

World War II in Europe started when Germany attacked
Poland in 1939; at that point, Britain and France declared war
on Germany. The Japanese attack of Pearl Harbour on December
7th, 1941, brought the United States into the war. The Japanese
fascist government was engaged in a war with China since its
invasion of Manchuria in 1931. German invasion of the Soviet
Union on June 22, 1941 completed the participants of the major
powers involved in World War II.

Putting aside actual estimates and statistics on the number
of military casualties during the two wars, taking into account
the extent of civilian casualties, incorporating the impact of
people dying from disease caused by the wars, it is fair to say
that the price paid by humanity is astounding, horrendous and
unimaginable.

There appears to be a consensus among statisticians that
Russia experienced the greatest military casualties in both
wars. It's worthwhile pointing out that Russia had 24 million
casualties compared to 418,500 American casualties in World
War II.[53] It is generally agreed that World War II was the deadli-
est military conflict in history, with an estimated 70-85 million
people perished.

Of great significance are two outcomes of World War II.
Firstly, the ugliness and horror of fascism was defeated and the
Axis powers' dream of achieving their empires was thwarted.[54]
However, people need to be vigilant to quash any resurgence
of the fascist menace, as there are many indicators pointing

---

53   https://www.nationalww2museum.org/students-teachers/student-
resources/research-starters

54   Ibid.

clearly to a resurgence, as manifested by white nationalism (i.e. Charlottesville white supremacist march, attacks on Jewish synagogues, election of Nazi-oriented leaders to Greek Parliament, the massacre in New Zealand by a so-called white nationalist).[55]

The nature of the second outcome is questionable and controversial in that a major superpower emerged, controlling what's ostensibly the greatest empire in history, surpassing by far Pac Romana and Pac Britannica—Pac Americana. It's generally known that the United States has hundreds of military bases situated in different parts of the world, from Southeast Asia, to Europe, to South America. People are at a loss to explain why the United States maintains such a vast network of military bases. Many scholars argue that the military bases are maintained to protect their vast colonial empire, in particular, to safeguard access to natural resources such as oil, natural gas and minerals.

The great concern is not only the colossal extent of Pac Americana, but the imperialist and military behaviour of the United States. The United States, under the influence of the military-industrial complex, with the collaboration of the puppet regime of Israel and its power structure, are propagating the culture of war and instability in the Middle East. The Middle East is a powder keg which could explode at any time. President Trump's approval of Israel transferring its capital to Jerusalem, followed by ratification of Israel taking control of the Golan Heights, adds more fuel to the fire burning in the Middle East.

According to Noam Chomsky, world-renowned author and fierce critic of Western foreign policy, has this to say: "The United States and Israel. The two major nuclear states in the world. I mean there's a reason why in international polls, run by US polling agencies, the United States is regarded as the greatest threat to world peace by an overwhelming margin. No other

---

55   Fascist doctrine will be explored in greater detail in Chapter 10.

country is even close. It's kind of interesting that the US media refused to publish this. But it doesn't go away."[56]

It's rather interesting and thought-provoking to observe American corporate media hurling accolades on Obama, praising him for being a recipient of the Nobel Peace Prize and lowering the threat of a nuclear holocaust. However, Obama's actions speak louder than his words. During the Obama presidency, many drones were released in a number of Middle Eastern countries, presumably targeting terrorist strongholds and leaders, killing many civilians considered collateral damage. Clearly, Obama, like his predecessor G.W. Bush, continued brutal militaristic ventures and unceasingly propagated a culture of war. The notion that Obama was motivated to lower the threat of war, thereby creating better conditions for a peaceful world, is total fallacy.

Perhaps the best evaluation of Obama's contribution to peace on a global basis is made by Noam Chomsky when he says: "Well actually he isn't. He's just initiated a trillion programme of modernization of US nuclear weapons system, which means expanding the nuclear weapon system. That's one of the reasons why the famous doomsday clock, established by the Bulletin of Atomic Scientists has, just a couple of weeks ago, been pushed two minutes closer to midnight. Midnight is the end. It's now three minutes from midnight. That's the closest it's been in 30 years, since the early Regan years when there was a major scare."[57]

The global community has no choice but to confront the ugliness of war and the existential threat of nuclear holocaust. Scholars, scientists and the public have come to the realization that there are no winners in a nuclear war. However, while reaching such a conclusion provides some psychological com-

56   Noam Chomsky on The Global Conversation. 2016.

57   Ibid.

fort, it merely reveals the superficial thinking that exists among the power brokers and leaders in the Western world.

Hopefully, the anti-war movement will step up its activity and gain momentum, focusing on exerting the necessary pressure on the leadership in the Western world, to take the initiative in working towards implementation of global total disarmament. There are now nine nations in possession of nuclear weapons, North Korea being the 9th nation, with the capacity to end life on the planet.

As a first step, it's incumbent on the international community to put pressure on the nuclear powers to cease further testing of nuclear weaponry. Cessation of nuclear testing would help create the mutual trust required if nuclear powers are to move forward towards a second step—establishing an agreement, framework and basis for implementing total world disarmament. Attainment of an agreement for total world disarmament would propel the nuclear powers to advance to the third and final step, which involves the organization of a comprehensive inspection and verification system.

If the global community will move in the direction of sanity and global disarmament remains to be seen; no one has the foresight to predict the future for humanity. However, writing is on the wall for homo sapiens; humanity needs to make a serious commitment and work unceasingly for the implementation of total disarmament or face the inevitable consequence of doomsday and extinction as mentioned by Noam Chomsky.[58]

---

58   Noam Chomsky, associated with Massachusetts Institute of Technology (MIT), was a famous linguist, philosopher, political activist and the author of hundreds of books.

CHAPTER 8

Empire-Building – From Prehistory to Modern Times

Neanderthal people existed for an estimated 35,000 years with no tribe threatening another with warfare and extinction. Archeological research and investigation of history tells us that primitive Neanderthal people lived a communal life and engaged in fishing, hunting and food gathering to survive. There were no organized social groups or social classes in existence with the aim of dominating another group. Evidence found in caves indicates that Neanderthal people were nomadic and moved from place to place as conditions changed. There are no definitive theories explaining the extinction of Neanderthal people.

Historians generally agree, in roughly 3500 B.C., new economic, social and political conditions arose, allowing for the genesis and development of a new form of society. Domestication of animals and establishment of agriculture led to the emergence of a new social and economic system. The nascent social and economic order provided an opportunity for the dominant social class to engage in conquests of other people and incorporate them into an empire. All ancient societies, often referred to as civilizations—Egyptian, Minoan, Roman and Greek—while civilized in a certain context, engaged in imperialistic conquests of other lands and enslavement of people. These ancient civilizations functioned as slave societies; slave labour was the basis of their economy. Imperial conquest and empire-building was the cornerstone of their foreign policies based on the ever-growing demand for slave production.

However, ancient civilizations experienced birth, development and glory, and like the Roman civilization and empire, they all collapsed. With the decline of the most recent ancient society, the Roman Western imperial empire in the latter part of the 5th century, Europe came under the sway of a different social and economic order, commonly referred to as feudalism.

Feudal society was also structured according to social classes with the aristocracy, the church being the dominant and governing social class and power structure. Unlike ancient civilizations, where the basis of the economy was slave production, economic productivity in the feudal economy relied on the labour of serfs. Serfs had a designated place in feudal society; a serf would reside upon and work a parcel of land owned by the lord of the manor. The serf possessed relative freedom compared to slavery; however, feudal regulations restricted his freedom of movement. He could not permanently leave his holding or his village without permission. Serfs worked on piece of land he resided on for three days of the week and three days on the estate of the landlord, the seventh day was the Sabbath, which allowed the serf and his family to attend church services. According to feudal laws, serfs were rigorously tied to their plot of land and were compelled to offer their unequivocal allegiance to the landlord and church official.

During the epoch of feudalism, empire-building and imperial ventures commonly occurred in Europe, and territorial holdings were frequently rearranged. Imperial ventures were limited to monarchs and emperors who had the allegiance of most noblemen and clergy. It wasn't until the 16th century, with the downfall of feudal society, introduction of new technology and new social and economic conditions, that the vista opened up for modern imperialism.

New inventions such as the compass, printing press, caravel, double entry system in accounting, weights and measurements and gun powder gave rise to mercantilism, a modern economic system known commonly as embryonic capitalism. In the new economic framework, the nascent merchant class, motivated by the profit motive, was destined to spearhead economic and social development among the newly-emerging nations, laying the foundation for modern imperialism.

As an economic system, mercantilism was organized to turn out finished products within the empire with minimal trade deficits. It included the fullest possible utilization of a nation's natural and human resources. Restrictions were placed on gold and silver exports and on importing commodities that could be made in sufficient supply and quality at home. The avaricious appetite for raw materials and cheap labour encouraged mercantilism to colonize new lands and people to be tightly controlled by the imperial nation. It led to a number of triangular systems, in which colonies could only sell to and buy from the ruling nation. This was likely the main reason why American colonies revolted against Britain.

In essence, the closed mercantilist economic philosophy fueled imperialism and later created conditions for the Industrial Revolution. Mercantilism was present during the 16th through 18th centuries when European nations—mainly Spain, Portugal, Britain, France, the Netherlands and Belgium—embarked on imperial ventures. Three nations in particular—Spain, France and Britain—built huge empires carved out of South and Central America, Africa and Asia.

Spanish and Portuguese colonialism was based on religious zeal, promoted by the Pope of the Catholic Church. The Pope exercised his authority to decree whole continents open to colonization by certain monarchs. Missionaries were sent by the church to convert Indigenous peoples to the Catholic faith. With arrival of conquistadores in the Americas, the process of anni-hilating the Amerindian was initiated, although diseases played a part.

David Stannard maintains that the "destruction of the Indians of the Americas was, by far and away, the most massive act of genocide in the history of the world... that the American Natives were deliberately and systematically exterminated over the course of several centuries and that the process continues to the present day."[59]

For three centuries after the arrival of Columbus in the Caribbean, the Spanish empire expanded across the Caribbean islands, half of South America and most of Central America, including Mexico.

According to David Eltis, areas controlled by the Spanish imperialists such as Mexico, Peru and large parts of Central America "used forced labour in mining activities."[60] However, depletion of Indigenous people on which labour-intensive plan-tations relied upon, propelled the plantation owners to search for labour elsewhere—they turned to the centuries-old barbaric slave trade of West Africa. The inhuman slave trade process began transporting African slaves across the Atlantic on a mas-sive scale. Large numbers of African people died in order to meet the demand for Spanish and Portuguese labour require-ments. Nearly a quarter of the African slaves died before they arrived at their destination.[61]

---

59   Stannard, David E. American Holocaust: *The Conquest of the New World.* Oxford University Press, 1993. p. 151.

60   Eltis, David. *Economic Growth and the Ending of the Transatlantic Slave Trade.* New York: Oxford University Press, 1987. p. 31.

61   Newson, Linda A. and Susie Minchin. *From Capture to Sale: The Portuguese Slave Trade to Spanish America in the Early Seventeenth Century.* Leiden: Brill, 2007. p. 72.

Both Spanish and Portuguese colonialists maintained constant and strict social monitoring and control over slavery. The goal of the plantation owners and other enterprises was sustaining a labour force at all times for economic production. The "money nexus" and the drive for profit led to a notorious period of history in the latter part of the 19th century and eve of World War I—the scramble for Africa (also known as the race for Africa or partition of Africa). The barbaric and inhuman process involved outright invasions, occupation and annexation of African territory by European nations and their inherent power structures, which signaled the new and modern imperialism.

Two European nations that were poised for empire-building in the 16th century—Britain, which was on fast track of establishing a colonial foothold, and France, which was similarly dreaming of laying claim to colonial territory in the new world. Both nations defied the papal decree on what territories could be settled.[62] Like Britain, France settled in the Americas—territory which is now Canada, the United States and some islands in the Caribbean. It wasn't long before the exclusively Iberian claims to the Americas was to be challenged by European nations such as Great Britain, France and the Netherlands. France built a colossal empire embodying three continents—the Americas, Africa and Asia. The overseas empire consisted of colonies and protectorates, as well as mandate territories, which came under French imperial rule starting in the 16th century. The French empire is historically divided into parts: first and second empire.

The first empire existed until the time of Bonaparte Napoleon (1815); the second empire lasted until it lost Indo-China in 1954 and then Algeria in 1962. At its apex, France was one of largest empires in history. Napoleon III played the greatest imperial

---

62   In 1493, Spanish-born Pope Alexander VI decreed all lands West of Cape Verde belonged to Spain, while all lands East belonged to Portugal.

role in expanding the second French empire. During his rule, the area of French overseas empire doubled in size.

Policies pursued by the power structure of French imperialism regarding its colonies was in harmony with the strategy of the Spanish and Portuguese regarding their Indigenous peoples. The conviction and belief of all three European powers was that the conquerors have divine and unequivocal rights over the lower races, and therefore have the sacred duty to civilize the inferior races.

The policies regarding Indigenous peoples being governed by Spanish, Portuguese and French imperial power structures had one thing in common—get as much surplus value out of their labour as possible in the shortest time possible. It must be stated and stressed that policies governing the Indigenous peoples of all three imperial powers were exploitative, brutal, inhuman, despicable and shameful to the white European race.

British imperialism, which also amassed vast territory and built an empire, earned the title Pac Britannica. Having defeated the Spanish armada in the latter part of the 16th century (1588), the British navy exercised command over the seas and was at liberty to engage in colonizing different parts of the world. By the turn of the 20th century, Great Britain controlled vast tracts of land and people in the Americas (now Canada and the United States), islands in the Caribbean, India, footholds in Africa, Australia and others—the empire was the most extensive and huge that history has ever seen.

To justify its imperialist and colonialist empire, Britain relied on such people as Rudyard Kipling, a poet and writer, who argued the burden had fallen on white men to civilize the lower races of Indigenous peoples. As stated by Rudyard Kipling, the British Empire was the Englishman's "Divine Burden to reign God's Empire on Earth and celebrate British Colonialism as a mission of civilization that would eventually benefit the colonized world."[63]

The implication of white man's burden was that the empire existed not for the benefit of Britain itself, but in order that primitive peoples, incapable of self-government, could eventually become civilized with British guidance.

Kipling argued that under colonial imperialism the moral burden falls on the white race divinely destined to civilize the brutish non-whites, who inhabit barbarous parts of the world. The Catholic and Protestant missionaries inherited the great challenge to displace the natives' religions with Christianity.[64]

However, Kipling, in his poetry and literature, aroused considerable negative reaction; there was a feeling among many people that "white man's burden" communicated excessively false noble intentions of Western colonialism for the non-white world.[65] But it was Kipling's engagement in jingoism which provoked contemporary poetic parodies that expressed serious moral outrage. The parodies critically dwelt on white supremacy and racism that underlie the philosophical basis and ideology of imperialism.

The story of imperialism would be somewhat limited if an attempt were not made to offer an explanation or a viable theory on the rise of civilizations in different historic epochs, examining why they became involved in empire-building.

Careful observation of past history seems to indicate that a common thread of imperialism weaves through identifiable epochs of history—the time of the ancient civilizations, period of feudalism and the epoch of modern history and market economies. It's somewhat perplexing and mind-boggling how a power

63   Langer, William. *A Critique of Imperialism*. New York: Council on Foreign Relations Inc., 1935. p. 6.

64   *Benet's Reader's Encyclopedia*. Fourth Edition, 1996. p. 1111-1112.

65   Ibid. p. 560.

structure, reflecting the dominant social class in society, would be capable of organizing the means necessary to bring different parts of the world under imperial rule. The most plausible thesis is that the power structure, with resources at its disposal provided by the propertied class, employed such techniques as demagoguery, skillful oratory and agitation among people, to gain support promoting a movement aimed at building an empire. Over time, the power structure destined to build an empire became firmly entrenched in society.

The newly constituted power structure,[66] based on the support of the propertied and dominant social class, arrived at a historic moment when it decided to launch its imperial forces and might to colonize and build an empire. This is illustrated historically by the power structures of ancient civilizations in their quest for territorial enlargement and enslavement of people. It's also true of empire-building in Europe during the feudal period, and it's clearly evident when European nations and their power structures, in the modern period of history (between 16th and 20th centuries) began carving up the world into their respective empires.

The 13 colonies in America engaged in the Revolutionary War (1775-1783) to gain its independence and the right to self-determination from Great Britain. Over a period of time, the colonies merged into the United States of America. In the latter part of the 19th century, it seems to have forgotten about its past anti-imperialist struggles against Great Britain. By the 1890's, the United States began flexing its muscles and adopted the "white man's burden" policy of imperialist expansion. The nascent American government and its power structure totally

---

66   The power structure of the ancient civilizations and European feudal society were not as elaborate as that of modern European nations; power structures of modern nations consist of a number of distinct elements: business tycoons, banks, military, secret service, corporate media, church and schools.

embraced imperialist principles. By the turn of the 20th century, the US understood the "white man's burden" to mean an implied justification for conquest and a mission of civilization that is ideologically connected to American "continental imperialist philosophy of manifest destiny." In 1902, following the American-Spanish war (1899-1902), the United States established geopolitical hegemony upon the islands and peoples in two hemispheres—the Philippines and Guam in the Pacific area, and Cuba and Puerto Rico in the Caribbean.[67]

It is necessary to point out that Social Darwinism, the theory of natural selection developed by Charles Darwin and popular in the United States in the late 19th century, merged with Herbert Spencer's sociological theory of racism. The merged theoretical outcome was perceived as justification for the practice of racism, laissez-faire doctrine and the evolutionary theory of mankind. With the Monroe Doctrine, the United States exercised hegemony over South and Central Americas and remained detached and unconcerned about Europe.

However, there was a dramatic shift in American foreign policy at the end of World War II. Shortly after the war, American imperialism sprang to life, unfurling its expansionist policies worldwide. While Britain and France were witnessing the collapse of their empires, the United States was busy establishing neocolonial footholds in many parts of the globe.[68]

While the United States propagandizes freedom and democracy across the globe, many would argue that, in reality, it is merely monitoring, policing and controlling its neocolonial

---

67   Butler, Charles Henry. The Treaty Making Power of the United States. The Banks Law Pub. Cor., 1902. p. 441.

68   It is estimated that the United States has roughly 800 military bases in foreign countries.

empire.[69] China, Russia and, to a degree, India are powerful economic, military and nuclear competitors of the United States. China is also making large investments in different parts of the world; however, unlike the United States, its regional investments do not involve building military bases.

In trying to understand 20th and 21st century imperialism, many scholars and individuals surmise about the intentions, purpose and reasons for the installation and existence of American military bases throughout the world. The official political line of American foreign policy is that the bases were installed with the consent of the nations, with the condition that they will be provided with economic aid and security. However, increasingly, people of the nations that have allowed military bases to be installed are questioning what the real motivation might be for installation of the bases. Recently, South Africa was approached by the United States, requesting permission to establish a military base on South African soil but was flatly refused.

However, one can posit the view that the real intention of the United States is not the provision of economic aid and security to nations consenting to installation of military bases, but rather to secure resources for multi-national corporations who are an integral part of the neocolonial American empire and monitored and controlled by the US' military-industrial complex (MIC).

All the evidence on imperialist behaviour of the United States suggests the military-industrial complex is the foundation of American neocolonialism and 21st century imperialism.[70]

---

69   Neocolonialism doesn't involve settlements, but promotes setting up military bases, allowing imperial power control over natural resources for transnational corporations, banks and financial agencies.

70   Dwight D. Eisenhower, in his farewell speech in 1961, warned the American people about the potential danger and threat posed by the military-industrial complex.

It's worth stating that President Trump appears to be a victim of narcissism but is allowed considerable latitude by the military-industrial complex to stage his Hollywood acting; however, there is reason to believe that if he should cross the line, he would be reigned in at the discretion of the military-industrial complex.

CHAPTER 9

Coming to Grips with Alienation

Evidence and logic clearly point to the fact man has an inherent duality—on the one side, man tends to be a social animal; on the other, man shows himself as a solitary being. By interacting with society, man appears to have great difficulty in achieving an equilibrium and be able to contribute to society. These two drives and their corresponding strength is fixed by inheritance, but the personality that emerges is essentially a reflection of the environment he lives in.

Nowadays, a typical individual has become more conscious than ever before of his dependence upon the society they live in; however, they don't experience this relationship as being a normal tie, but rather as a threat to their natural rights and livelihood. Under capitalism, selfish drives of their psychological make-up are constantly being accentuated, while their social drives begin to deteriorate over time. Human beings in society, whatever their social position, suffer from this process of social dehumanization, not realizing they are prisoners of their own egotism. They feel insecure and deprived of the decent, simple and unsophisticated enjoyment in life and feel isolated, lonely, disconnected and alienated.

People in today's society are increasingly speaking out about the feelings of isolation and loneliness which they are experiencing, especially seniors. Most disturbing is that the meaning and purpose of life has become muddled and unclear. The corporate media propagates consumption and material aggrandizement as being the road to happiness. People try to put things in some meaningful form in reaction to the prevalence of the confusion and uncertainty that exists. Hence, it's necessary to examine the concept of estrangement or alienation in some detail.

Alienation refers to individuals who feel isolated from other people and are denied opportunities from participating in societal activities that other people do. Individuals who consider themselves or are perceived by other people as out of place, or appear to be outsiders or misfits in society, will conclude that they are unwelcome and are destined to feel the full weight of alienation.

Scholars on the subject of alienation tend to agree that human beings, by embracing the real world with their physical and mental powers, cannot be fully understood without analyzing and understanding the role of alienation in society. Human history is increasingly more complex in its development, effecting increased frustration and alienation. It's important to note that an alienated being has great difficulty in grasping how the real world functions and understanding nature when people around him remain antagonistic and alien to him.

Historically, Western thought on the issue of alienation and idolatry can be traced back to the Scriptures of the Old Testament. Writings on alienation can also be found in the writings of St. Augustine.The deadness and emptiness of the idol is clearly expressed in the Old Testament: "eyes they have, but do not see; ears they have but do not hear." Unfortunately, the more people relegate their power and individuality to the idols, the poorer and more estranged they become. Human beings can be enticed to idolize the state, church, person and possessions; above all, human beings fail to realize that man's fight against God is, in reality, a fight against the idol that is called God.

People tend to share the messianic hope of the prophets of the old testament and spiritual roots of humanism embedded in

Greek and Roman thinking. Messianic hope constitutes a primary feature of occidental thinking. Most of the Old Testament prophets share the idea that history has meaning—that man perfects himself in the process of history and that he will eventually create a society of peace and justice.

After the Reformation period, messianic thinking was no longer expressed in religious thought but was expressed in the Enlightenment period of English and French revolutions. However, the full messianic thinking was expressed by Marxist Socialism that was aroused by Spinoza, Goethe and Hegel. It's important to remind ourselves, what is common to 13th century Christian thought, 18th century enlightenment and 19th century socialism is the concept that state and spiritual values cannot be separated—that politics and moral values are inextricably linked.

Following the Renaissance period and subsequent Western imperial conquests, wealthy elites in society, obsessed with power and material aggrandizement, engaged in manipulation of man and the promotion of alienation among the masses. An alienated man worships things he creates himself and, in so doing, transforms himself into a thing; more so, he is in touch with himself only by worshipping an idol and in the process becomes estranged from his own life forces and becomes a victim of idols.

In the modern period of history, Hegel coined the concept of alienation and considered that "the history of man was, at the same time, the history of man's alienation."[71] Both Hegel and Marx professed that it was important to make a distinction between existence and essence (man's nature); man, according to them, was alienated from his essence. As Fromm placed it,

---

71   Fromm, Eric. *Marx's Concept of Man.* p. 47.

"man is not what he ought to be, and that he ought to be, that what he could be."[72]

With industrialization of Europe, alienation in the capitalist market economy became the norm. Following the thinking of Hegel, and continued by Marx, the process of alienation in modern Europe is featured in work and division of labour.[73]

A working man connects with nature, but with the emergence of capitalism, based on the legal foundation of private property, and with the concomitant development of division of labour, labour tends to lose its character of being an expression of man's powers. At work, man fails to realize his potential by being denied self-actualization; he develops a feeling of misery rather than well-being and becomes exhausted and mentally debased. Being disconnected from humanity and denied the opportunity for self-actualization makes the individuals see themselves, or be seen by other people, as simply an object or entity in the system of production.

The process of alienation influences the lives of working people in a number of ways, most of which are negative and unfavourable. When a working person is distanced from what he is creating, he is no longer considered an active member of society; on the contrary, he is considered a tool to be manipulated and controlled by those above him. In such circumstances, the worker is transformed from being a creative member in society into a commodity—a reflection of supply and demand and is bought and sold in a market economy like a loaf of bread.

The worker feels himself at home only during his time off and leisure occasions, while at work he feels homeless and estranged. In a capitalist market economy, man is alienated from his own creative powers in that the products of his work become alien entities and eventually overtake him. As stated by

---

72   Ibid. p. 47.

73   Capital 1, 1. C. p. 536.

Marx, "The laborer exists for the process of production, and not the process of production for the laborer."[74]

There is an ongoing debate in the left-wing movement whether socialism should only be concerned with redistribution and more equalization of income, or should socialism be focused on liberation of man from the type of work which destroys his individuality, of both worker and employer by their own making? Kierkegaard and Marx were not so much concerned with equalization of income as they were engrossed with the mode of production and the liberation of man from the kind of work which destroys his unique personality.

Interestingly, Albert Einstein has this to say about the impact of capitalism on the individual: "Unlimited competition leads to a huge waste of labour, and to that crippling of the social consciousness of the individual... this crippling of individuals, I consider the worst evil of capitalism. Our whole educational system suffers from this evil. An exaggerated competitive attitude is inculcated into the student, who is trained to worship acquisitive success as a preparation for his future career."[75]

Einstein further elaborates what the impact on individuals is likely to be in a socialist society:"The education of the individual, in addition to promoting his own innate abilities, would attempt to develop in him a sense of responsibility for his fellow men in place of the glorification of power and success in our present society."[76]

Einstein presents a powerful case when he argues that if man is to overcome the forces that promote alienation, fundamental institutional changes are required in society (i.e. social relations reflecting a new social and economic order would need to be established). However, he cautions about change in the

---

74   Ibid.

75   Einstein, Albert. "Why Socialism." Monthly Review, 1949.

76   Ibid.

economy when he says the establishment of a planned economy is not yet socialism. Einstein warns that a planned economy as such may be accompanied by the complete enslavement of individuals.[77]

Einstein points out, and socialists generally agree, that achievement of socialism necessitates resolving some perplexing and extremely difficult socio-political issues (i.e. political and economic centralization could easily lead to bureaucratic control, thus, protection of human rights are a critical issue). Clarity and further understanding of complex issues need to be explored if socialist ideas are to advance.

Many socialists tend to adopt the Marxist view that the working class is the most alienated segment of the population; however, Eric Fromm posits the view that that's no longer the case. He argues that alienation is the fate of the vast majority of people, and that it's no longer only machines but manipulation of symbols and man. The vast diversified workers in modern industry and society, be they clerks, salesmen, office workers, or executive personnel and others, idolize one thing in the main—the corporation—and these people are more alienated than the manual worker.[78] The big question is: Will a docile and frightened mankind be saved from the power of the things it has created—the two existential threats, environmental and nuclear disaster.

---

77   Ibid.

78   Fromm, Eric. *Marx's Concept of Man*. p. 57.

CHAPTER 10

Three Basic Ideologies – Capitalism, Fascism and Socialism

Capitalism

One can project and test a simple hypothesis: Do most Canadians know what neoliberalism is? When one meets some friends in a coffee shop and asks them, "What is neoliberalism?" the most likely response will be "I have no idea."

The reason is that neoliberalism in Canada, and generally in the Western world, is kept silent and in the dark. Academics or the politically-inclined may have heard of the term and have some knowledge of it, but the vast majority will not recognize the term. By and large, there is a black-out of neoliberalism in Western society. It's rather strange that an ideology which dominates and shapes the lives and thinking in Western society is so shrouded in secrecy and mystery and remains largely nameless.

A plausible explanation for the black-out of neoliberalism is that it's intentionally and strategically kept in the dark because it's advantageous to the dominant social class and its power structure in society. When major crises or scandals occur, it stands to reason that the dominant social class and the corporate elite are off the hook—society can't point fingers at who is responsible. For example, in reference to the Panama Papers scandal, the 2007-2008 economic meltdown or the alienation dilemma in society, can one rationally implicate neoliberalism?

In reality, neoliberalism is so deeply entrenched and pervasive in the Western world that, even if one happened to stumble into it, one would not recognize it, let alone define it. The term neoliberalism was first defined in Paris in 1938 by Ludwig Von Mises and Frederick Hayek.[79] Neoliberalism arose out of classical liberalism, based on the works of John Locke and Adam Smith, which became the basis of Western political philosophy. The most important principle extolled by classical liberalism was liberty—the idea that every person has the right to life, freedom and happiness. The American and French revolutions incorporated John Locke's principle on human rights into their revolutionary struggles.

Neoliberalism as an ideology places considerable emphasis on laissez-faire economics. While compatible with classical liberalism economically, it tends to focus much more on the market economy rather than human rights. As an ideology, neoliberalism places its emphasis on free market competition, based on the premise that there be minimal restrictions on the capitalist market economy. Apologists of neoliberalism argue that any attempt to restrict competition by government regulations interferes with the market economy and is inimical, not only to the productive process, but is detrimental to human freedom and liberty.

According to capitalism, democratic capitalism, classical liberalism, neoliberalism and any other type of capitalist "ism", the role of government should be closely monitored and scrutinized; moreover, taxation and government regulations should be substantially restricted, and targeted public institutions and services should be privatized. Privatization or reprivatisation,

---

79   See Frederick Hayek's *The Road to Serfdom and Ludwig Von Mises' Bureaucracy.*

now a hallmark of neoliberalism and capitalism, first gained its prominence in Nazi Germany where capitalist property remained sacrosanct. Trade unions are perceived as an anachronism in society working contrary to the operation of winners and losers in society.

Unequivocally, neoliberalism holds the view that the market economy, being the foundation of capitalism, is the panacea to a productive economy where everyone receives what he earns and deserves. An attempt to create a more equal society is counterproductive, regressive and contrary to human nature. Unlike a planned or more equitable society, an unequal society based on competition, which is an inherent feature of a capitalist market economy, generates untold wealth which trickles down to enrich everyone.

In the post-war period, Keynesian economic policies were widely applied, but by the 1970s, the policies of Keynes began to plummet—neoliberalism surfaced and entered the mainstream of economic activity. During the Thatcher and Reagan era, policies of neoliberalism were aggressively promoted via massive corporate tax reductions, extensive privatization of public services, wide-spread deregulation, suppression of trade unions and more.

However, upon closer examination, the changes orchestrated by neoliberalism meant, in reality, that the majority of workers and wage earners would experience a major economic hit. Tax cuts for the wealthy meant decreasing purchasing power for ordinary folk; privatization of public services meant greater profits for the rich; extensive deregulation would mean more rivers to be polluted and endangering the environment. In short, the changes promoted by neoliberalism and its power structure are nothing less than a masquerade or a smoke-screen for capitalism—a green light provided to corporate interests for generating more profit and wealth. It needs to be stressed that those who own and operate privatized or semi-privatized services derive incredible fortunes, by investing a minimum and imposing exceptional rent or fees (i.e. oligarchs in many capitalist countries take advantage of opportunities by acquiring public or state assets at fire-sale prices). It turns out that the market under neoliberalism and capitalism works in a mysterious way; in reality, what the market wants tends to be what the corporations and owners want.

Neoliberalism, a disguised form of capitalism, was characterized by two authors: Frederick Hayek and Ludwig Van Mises. Both authors argued that government planning takes away initiative and freedom, and leads society inexorably to a totalitarian regime. However, the invective hurled by Hayek and Mises at those who subscribe to government planning are groundless in that capitalistic nations, operating largely under the secret banner of neoliberalism, are in reality practising a secret form of totalitarianism. Casting aspersions on the concept of government planning, based on the notion that some societies have unsuccessfully applied planning, does not necessarily mean the process of planning is unworkable and flawed. Such nations as China, Cuba and formerly the Soviet Union adopted the concept of planning in their economies; the USSR collapse does not mean that planning is unworkable. The fact remains that the Soviet Union was engaged in some extraordinary planning to defeat a formidable enemy in World War II: Nazi Germany. Furthermore, it's rather difficult to build a society based on public ownership and planning when several powerful hostile nations are determined to see that public enterprise and public planning fail.

A significant section of society in many Western nations contain social institutions which rely on extensive planning—hospitals, libraries, universities, healthcare, social agencies, etc.—one will notice that they are designated as social or public institutions, but not socialist; one wonders why they are not called socialist. Undoubtedly, there are inefficiencies in the planning process of many of these social institutions; however, the inadequacies of the planning activities are preferable to privatization and profiteering.

There are some disturbing signs in the American republic. Although it's under the influence of neoliberalism, which Trump never refers to by name, close observation of American society indicates, despite frequent references to human rights in the Constitution, there is disturbing evidence that the United States is drifting towards an unknown. Under the Trump administration, the United States appears to be in a quagmire; it continues to police the world and engage in costly wars abroad. On the other hand, it's domestic policies, particularly its policies in relation to illegal immigrants, are in a state of disarray.

What's rather disturbing is that high-finance institutions such as IMF, World Bank and World Trade Organization are using their clout to impose the ideology of neoliberalism on a large section of the world. Informed observers tell us that the Western world is facing serious stagnation. All Western (G7) countries show a 1.3 % growth comparable to the Great Depression of the 1930's. Labour share of income, except for the 1%, is declining dramatically; national investment, which is normally the engine of the economy is stagnating, and income and wealth inequality is soaring.[80]

Sooner or later, hopefully much sooner, the disguised mask of neoliberalism will be shattered and a true portrayal of the economic power base will be revealed—the role of capitalist power structure, of oligopolies, monopolies, plutocrats and banks. Both Keynesian and neoliberal economics are destined to eclipse. Time will tell whether a new economic model and a new design will emerge amenable to the 21st century; the new model predicated on arresting the global suicidal drift towards an environmental disaster or nuclear holocaust.

---

80   Foster, Bellamy. "The Plight of the U.S. Working Class." *Monthly Review* 65, No. 8 (January 2014). p. 1-22.

Fascism

Fascism is resurging in a new ideological form in different parts of the globe. It should not be considered a mere aberration or anomaly; on the contrary, it has been shown historically to be as one of the important forms of political organization, espoused and subtly utilized by dominant social classes in the developed capitalist part of the world.[81]

In the early part of the 20th century, fascist ideologies and regimes took hold via a number of leaders: Hirohito in Japan, Franco in Spain, Mussolini in Italy and Hitler in Germany. In today's world, with a noticeable resurgence of fascist movements, albeit still on a small scale, they nevertheless pose a serious threat to humanity in a world of confusion and uncertainty. The instability of the world gives us no choice but to monitor populous movements to determine if any conditions have developed that are conducive to fascist development. It's important to examine fascist ideology, focusing on German Nazism in particular, in an effort to determine what conditions allow fascism to attain political power.

There are a variety of theories and views on how and why fascist movements attain dictatorial power. Many informed individuals posit the view that fascism arises out of deteriorating capitalist social and economic conditions. The inherent business cycle under capitalism inevitably causes a downturn in the economy, precipitating a major economic depression. Concentration of wealth at the top literally means diminution of purchasing power below; jobs become more scarce, and the rise in unemployment creates ideal conditions for a fascist movement to resurge. Fascist organizers, relying on demagoguery and agitation among the people, who are experiencing dastardly economic and social conditions, capture the support of people at

---

81   Amin, Samir. "The Return of Fascism in Contemporay Capitalism." *Monthly Review* 66, No. 4 (Sep 2014). p. 1-12.

the bottom of the social ladder. In short, it's capitalism that gives birth to fascism; it's not human nature or man's innate depravity that drives people in the direction of fascism. When unfavourable social and economic conditions are created under capitalism, a well-organized fascist organization, using a well-thought strategy, and led by a charismatic leader and demagogue, is in a position to attain political power.

Fascism does not threaten the capitalist social and economic order; contrarily, it extols, promotes and safeguards the wealthy propertied social class. Fascists support a capitalist state-controlled and regulated economy. As pronounced by Adolf Hitler,"We stand for the maintenance of private property... We shall protect free enterprise as the most expedient, or rather the sole possible economic order."[82]

Property rights are safeguarded under Nazi rule except for those targeted racially, sexually or politically whose property is confiscated to benefit the wealthy. Nazi ideology aims at a dictatorship—a totalitarian state, organized around a tight and centralized executive. Fascism is one of the possible political forms which capitalism may assume in the monopoly and imperialist phase of capitalist development.[83]

It's important to underscore the basic social and economic structure of capitalism under fascist rule remains unchanged; the dominant social class is assured of non-interference in its economic affairs. The prime objective of a fascist state is to repress and discipline the population while, at the same time, protecting and promoting capitalist property relations (i.e. providing conditions for increased profit and capital accumulation). While the economy is being stabilized, plans and a strategy are being developed for territorial and imperial expansion.

---

82   Heiden, Konrad. Der Furhrer. Boston: Houghton Mifflin, 1944. p. 287.

83   Sweezy, Paul and Paul A. Baran. *Monopoly Capital: An Essay on the American Economic and Social Order*. New York: Monthly Review Press, 1966.

It's necessary to point out that, during Hitler's rise to power, dominant parts of the economy were state-owned (i.e. steel, coal, ship-building and banking industries were largely nationalized). However, Hitler's privatization policies enhanced profiteering and consolidation of the Nazi regime. As stated by Wicos Poulantzas, "Nazism maintained juridical regulation in matters of the protection of the capitalist order and private property."[84]

Privatization under the Nazi regime brought about the final destruction of the liberal democratic order. The policy of "Gleichschaltung" was implemented, bringing people into line by ideological propaganda, intimidation, forced cooperation or simply coercion. The overall strategy of Gleichschaltung was to promote purity of race and unity of Nazi movement.[85]

Turning to current and contemporary development in the Western world, with a focus on the United States, one is enticed to ask the question: Are there any signs indicating that the United States under Donald Trump's leadership is moving in an uncharted and questionable direction? A different form of fascism requires a new form and approach to "Gleichschaltung" in effort to bring all institutions and people into line.

It's of great interest and a challenge to understand the real intent of Trump's "America First" policy, unfurled in his inaugural address, which was noticeably ultra-nationalism, aimed not at domination of Europe and its colonies (as was the case of Nazi Germany) but in restoring US primacy over the globe—leading to a potentially deadly phase of imperialism.[86] Especially disturbing is the thinking of Trump that anthropogenic climate change is a hoax and doesn't exist, defying global scientific consensus. Myron Ebell, head of the Competitive Enterprises

---

84   Poulantzas, Wicos. *Fascism and Dictatorship.* London: Verso, 1974. p. 344,

85   Schmitt, Carl. "The Legal Basis of the Total State." Griffin ed., Fascism p. 138-139.

86   See Donald Trump's inaugural address. January 20, 2017.

Institute, a major speaker for climate denial and a key Trump adviser on environment, has declared the environmental movement "the greatest threat to freedom and prosperity in the modern world"; he attacked climate scientists with the aim of removing them from government.[87] Ebell went so far as to characterize the Pope's encyclical on climate change as "leftist drivel"[88] It's sad, serious and unfortunate that Trump seems to be ready to transgress all legal norms to submerge, degrade and discredit environmentalism. Some well-informed observers argue that the United States is in a pre-fascist historic mode and that the White House tends to display neo-fascist leanings.

All new fascist movements focus on ultra-nationalism, xenophobia, racism and territorial expansion by military means. With the collapse of the Soviet Union in 1990, the United States used the power gap opportunity to engage in its imperial regime change policy (i.e. Iraq, Libya, Syria and Afghanistan), and the policy of regime change is still in play.

It was Hitler and Nazi Germany who first introduced Keynesian economic stimulus through military spending, privatization, destruction of unions and initiating cuts in workers' wages.[89]

There is a need for people in democratic societies to keep an eagle eye on nascent ultra-right movements that are emerging globally. The Charlottesville ultra-nationalist and white supremacist parade and the election of a small number of ultra-nationalists to Greek Parliament is a wake-up call for people who believe in freedom, substantive democracy and human dignity.

87   Carrington, Damien. "Green Movement Greatest Threat to Freedom." *The Guardian*. January 30, 2017.

88   Fountain, Henry. "Myron Bell takes on the EPA." *The New York Times*. November 11, 2016.

89   Kalecki, Michal. *The Last Phase in the Transformation of Capitalism*. New York: Monthly Review Press, 1972. p. 65-73.

Many observers are of the strong opinion that the deteriorating social and economic conditions in the capitalist Western world are a breeding ground for the emergence of ultra-nationalist and extreme right-wing movements. In short, classical liberalism, neoliberalism, democratic capitalism and private enterprise capitalism—call it what you will—all are being placed under the microscope in effort to discover the disease and conditions that spur the birth and rise of fascism. The erratic behaviour of Donald Trump, the confusion and uncertainty propagated by his movement and the noticeable fascist leanings being displayed, are worrisome, troublesome and frightening.

Socialism

Social media in the Western world is engaged in a deep and widespread vilification and degradation of the ideology of socialism and socialist ideas. Despite the popularity of Bernie Sanders' concept of socialism in the United States and some recognition that's given to socialists in the British Labour Party, the corporate world in the West maintains the commanding heights in characterizing socialism as being something next to evil.

The power structures or elites, representing the dominant social classes, carefully monitor socialist tendencies and developments and react to them accordingly. The United States in particular keeps a sharp eye on any nation that shows signs of socialist activity. For example, the US' harassment and interference in the national affairs of Venezuela is a violation of international law and the UN charter. It will be interesting to observe how the Venezuelan situation plays out.

The greatest fear Britain, France and the United States have is the possible emergence of socialism. On the other hand, socialists are concerned about enormous profits and capital that's being accumulated by oligopolies such as the insurance industry, drug companies, manufacturing and armaments industry and oil companies of the three nations mentioned. It's common knowledge that in the past 30 years, wages in these three nations reflect a plateau and virtually no increase. On the other hand, profits and capital accumulation of the top 1% rose sharply or logarithmically.[90]

It's important to highlight the fact that the corporate media is inexorably silent or simply ignores the positive role that social institutions play in society. It's indisputable that the social sector, encompassing the numerous social institutions of the nations mentioned, represent a substantive portion of the economy.

The Canadian economy displays a vast array of social institutions ranging from universities, colleges, libraries and schools to the medicare system, public housing, credit unions, etc. Interestingly, public institutions are referred to as "social institutions" and not "socialist"; undoubtedly, for the reason that the dominant social class cannot tolerate the term "socialist" to be popularized in Canadian society. Under capitalism, the system operates according to the principles of the market economy and private enterprise minimizes any reference to socialism. There exists a critical difference in the modus operandi of social institutions and private enterprise institutions. The prime motivation of social institutions is to provide services to the public as efficiently as possible; on the other hand, the main motivation of corporate institutions and private enterprise is to accumulate as much money as possible, and as quickly as possible, via the legalized profit system. The "money nexus" under capitalism is considered to be an institutional norm.

Since corporations use their capital in a free enterprise market economy to accumulate capital and wealth via the mechanism of profit, the inevitable result of this process is the concentration of excessive wealth at the top 1%.[91] At some point, corporations inexorably engage in a series of economic battles with labour over wages, social benefits and profit sharing. However,

90   Foster, Bellamy. "The Plight of the U.S. Working Class."

91   Ibid.

the conflict between capital and labour is only temporarily resolved; the basic contradiction between the two antagonistic parties continues to rankle.

A number of informed observers argue that fundamental institutional change is on the horizon—implementation of a new form of economic and social relations, namely socialism, has become an objective necessity.

What is the origin of socialism? What is its philosophy? Is it feasible for the new millennium?

The first current of socialist thinking was under the name of "utopian socialism" in the mid-19th century in Europe and was popularized by Saint-Simon, Fourier, Proudhon and Owen. They propagated the view that if capital and corporations would voluntarily relinquish its ownership of the means of production to the state or workers, unemployment and poverty could be abolished. However, it wasn't long before utopian socialist idealism had eclipsed into disfavour and irrelevance.

It was in the latter part of the 19th century that Karl Marx and Frederick Engels reasserted realistic premises of socialist ideas based on science and empirical studies. To distinguish themselves from utopian socialism, Marx and Engels adopted the word "communism" as the name for their nascent ideology. Unlike the utopian socialists, who Marx and Engels described as being too idealistic, their communist theory for building socialism was based on empirical and scientific thinking. Marxism gained a large following in the late 19th century, the high point being the October Russian Revolution in the early 20th century.

At this point, its proper to mention some of the prominent communist leaders and Marxist writers of the 20th century: Marx, Engels, Lenin, Martov , Trotsky, Mao-Zedong, Castro, Guevara, Fromm, Einstein and Noam Chomsky.

The concept of socialism, based on realism under the new, ideological name of communism, was introduced and popularized by Marx and Engels. They advanced the view that utopia socialists displayed honourable intentions but fell into the trap of idealism and lacked a practical strategy for realization of socialism.

For a workable and realistic strategy, Marx and Engels proposed that workers necessarily need to organize to win political power, preferably by peaceful means if possible, but by force or revolutionary action if necessary. The newly established state, working in conjunction with workers and the people, will unfold the socialist (public ownership) mode of production, which according to Marx is a necessary preparatory stage for the transition to communism. During the socialist phase, workers would work according to their ability and be rewarded according to their contribution, meaning there would be a wage differential. Upon the arrival of the phase of communism, workers would work according to their ability and be rewarded according to their need.[92]

The attempt of the Soviet Union to build socialism lasted nearly three quarters of a century before its collapse; on the other hand, China and Cuba are still functioning as communist states. China has deviated markedly from Marxist orientation; whether China will revert in its policies to authentic Marxist principles remains to be seen. Cuba is struggling to maintain its form of socialism amid American potential threat and its revived economic block-aid. Venezuela is another nation which is desperately struggling to sustain its form of socialism, much to the displeasure of the United States. Again, time will tell how American interference in Venezuela, clearly a violation of international law, will be played out.

---

92 People who subscribe to socialist thinking, but not Marxist thinking, dismiss the attainability of communism as being idealistic and wishful thinking, while Marxist socialists argues that the stage of communism is desirable and achievable. Marx posited the view that society would develop beyond the mere equalization of wages and income and liberate man from alienation, which was the main goal of communism.

It's necessary to make a cursory reference to the collapse of the Soviet Union, in that an ongoing debate still continues for its decline. Many observers dwell on two factors as being the basis for the decline and eclipse of the Soviet Union: firstly, immediately following World War II, the Truman doctrine was launched and the Soviet Union, formerly a war ally, suddenly became an evil enemy and the Cold War began. According to G.F. Kennan, strategist for promoting the collapse of the Soviet Union, architect of the "containment theory of communism", based his theory on the premise that the Soviet Union could be dismantled by encircling it with military bases. Encirclement would create sufficient economic and social stress, leading to the collapse of the Soviet Union.[93]

Secondly, a contributing factor to the Soviet collapse was the disconnect which developed during the Cold War between the Communist Party leadership and the population. The role of Soviets, which Lenin talked about during and shortly after the revolution, over time became dysfunctional. During the Cold War, Soviets functioned largely in name only. Severing of the party nexus with the people, intense American military harassment and encirclement of the Soviet Union made the collapse of the Soviet Union inevitable.

In examining the different tendencies and socialist formulations, it is essential to turn to the phenomenon of social democracy and social democratic parties in Europe. Blair of England, Mitterrand of France and Schroeder of Germany all portrayed themselves as social democrats, but on occasion would inadvertently make reference to socialism. Interestingly, during their terms in office, none of them made an attempt to implement any serious socialist policies. The New Democratic Party of Canada, which officially dropped the word "socialism", has joined its

---

93   "The Sources of Soviet Conduct." *Foreign Affairs* 25, No. 4 (1947). p. 566-582.

counterparts in Europe as being another reformist social democratic party.

Turning to our neighbour to the South, there appears to be a noticeable shift to the left in the American democratic party. A number of people, in addition to Bernie Sanders, articulate the need for socialist policies in the United States. However, there still are the democrats of the old guard, who claim to be democrats but wear republican clothing, and who in reality have a vested interest in perpetuating the status quo.

With the Trump phenomenon, the United States appears to be in a state of confusion and uncertainty; even more so, Dr. Richard Wolff argues that the United States is on a path bound to experience a serious long-term social and economic downturn.[94]

There is a way out of the crisis for the United States, but it needs to exercise foresight and audacity to change direction in its domestic and foreign policies. In an effort to offset the domestic immigration crisis, the answer is not to cut off aid to Guatemala, El Salvador and Honduras, since it will only exacerbate the problem of immigration; on the contrary, a viable long-term policy for the United States would be to provide loans to those nations at low interest rates to be paid back over a negotiated time. The critical condition of the loan would be that the recipient nations of the loan would be obliged to buy factory component parts from the US, which are required for building their industry. Such a trade agreement is fair and a two-way street—it is good for the United States since it would provide export opportunities for its commodities; equally, it would be beneficial to Central American nations for the job opportunities that the trade relationship would provide. Critics of the proposal argued the plan is too idealistic and impractical; however, some observers say the proposal suggested, or a similar trade agree-

---

94   Wolff, Richard. *Capitalism's Crisis Deepens.*

ment, would greatly assist the United States to make a sustained transition from a deeply entrenched militarized economy to a domestic welfare economy, based on peace and not war.

Noam Chomsky contrasts military spending with welfare or social spending and how it affects the US economy. He argues that social spending could have the same "pump-priming" effect as military spending; however, there is a fundamental difference between social pump-priming and military priming. According to Chomsky, extraordinary military spending effects minimum structural changes in society, while public works and social spending maximizes changes in the economy by creating new institutions, redistributes income and promotes a democratizing impact on society.[95]

Making a distinction between the two forms of spending is noteworthy, but what's lacking is a proposal which would encourage and entice the military industry to cut back on military spending and channel its resources for social spending. As suggested previously, long-term loans and equitable trade relationships with third world countries is a way out of the economic debacle for the United States and its allies.

Finally, it is fair to say that rational, peace-loving people and socialists of all stripes would gladly support diversion of military spending to social and welfare spending. It's in keeping with the need to work for total disarmament in effort to avert a nuclear holocaust.

---

95   "Horror Beyond Description: Noam Chomsky on the Latest Phase of War on Terror." https://truthout.org/articles/horror-beyond-description-noam-chomsky-on-the-latest-phase-of-the-war-on-terror/

CHAPTER II

Democracy and Freedom in the Western World

Canadians and Europeans, under the influence of neoliberalism, extol the Western version of democracy and freedom quite openly and boldly. As do European nations, Canada places great emphasis on the right to private property, minimal intervention of government in the economy and unrestricted competition in an unfettered market economy. The institution of private property is closely guarded by neoliberalism and is construed as a sacred economic freedom in society. Politically, apologists of Western democracies stress the existence of multiple political parties, which operate openly and freely as compared to some modern societies which display the one-party state. However, a one-party state doesn't necessarily mean that less democracy is being practised, since they hold elections and elect representatives to parliament as they do in multi-party states. Western democracies also place great emphasis on various other rights and freedoms which are entrenched in the Charter of Rights.

It's of interest to note how Western democracies interpret and characterize democracy and freedom. It would appear that neoliberalism, which is a cornerstone of Western democracy, finds it difficult or doesn't see the need to delve deeper to arrive at a better understanding of democracy and freedom and what they really ought to mean.

A better understanding of the meaning and relationship between democracy and freedom necessitates closer observation and examination of the origin and development of the two inextricably linked concepts. Inevitably, it means tracing history back to the Greek classical period, when Greek city-states functioned. Of particular interest is the city-state of Athens, where democracy and freedom had its origin.

Greece, during the early classical period of history, was an amorphous collection of independent city-states called "poleis", many of which were oligarchies. The term "democracy" first appeared in ancient Greek political and philosophical thought in the city-state of Athens during antiquity. In 507 B.C., Cleisthenes introduced a series of political reforms which he called "demokratia"—rule by the people.[96] Democracy is derived from the Greek word "demokratia" which was coined from "demos", meaning people, and "kratos", meaning rule. Democracy was used in the early Greek classical period to denote the political systems that existed in some Greek city-states, including Athens.

The government of Athens was based on three main pillars: Assembly of the Demos, Council of 500 and the Peoples' Court. Athenian democracy in real life took the form of direct democracy. It involved random selection of citizens to fill government administrative and judicial positions. The legislative assembly consisted of eligible Athenian citizens who were allowed to speak and vote in the Assembly, which set the laws for the state of Athens.

In taking a closer look at the concept of democracy, it is fair to say that Athens took a significant but small step on the long road to democracy. Undoubtedly, people were brought together

---

96   Cleisthenes was an ancient Greek lawgiver largely responsible for reforming Athenian constitution and setting it on a limited democratic footing.

to engage in discussion and deliberation; however, the unfortunate part is that the citizen gathering or assembly consisted primarily of landowners, affluent merchants and propertied people. It may be more appropriate to designate what Athenians claimed as democracy to be, in reality, a plutocracy. Historical evidence clearly indicates that most people were denied participation in the Assembly and exercising *demokratia*. For example, women, slaves, foreigners, non-landowners and men under 20 years were barred from participating in the democratic process.

Hence, when reference is made to Athenian democracy, one needs to tread carefully not to exaggerate or mis-characterize the extent to which democracy was practised in Athenian society. In reality, the dominant social class, consisting of rich landowners and a numerically small but vocal and powerful merchant class, shaped and determined the social and economic policies of Athenian society. More often than not, demagogues and orators would have a field day at the assembly meetings, swaying the thinking of citizenry in a certain direction.

However, it should be stated that although Athenian *demokratia* existed for only two centuries, innovations implemented by Cleisthenes, who came to be known as the father of Athenian democracy, was one of Greece's most interesting and beneficial contributions to humanity.

Following the decline of ancient civilizations and the eclipse of Athenian democracy, Europe entered a period of history known as the Dark Ages and characterized by feudalism. During the epoch of feudal relations (from roughly 500-1500), political power and decision-making was vested entirely in the nobility, clergy and monarchy. Democracy was essentially absent and virtually unknown in the medieval world. The only people who might have been acquainted with Athenian democracy would be such personalities as Seneca, Saint Augustine or Saint Thomas Aquinas. In sum, characterizing life in the feudal society, one can say that life of the serf population was simple, difficult and humble; on the other hand, the knights enjoyed an exciting, romantic and chivalrous living, while nobility led a comfortable and leisurely life compared to the ascetic and solitary life of the clergy.

By the 13th century, a semblance of parliamentary democracy can be noted, when English kings met with the baronial class, hoping to acquire money from barons for fighting wars, mostly against Scotland. According to the Magna Carta of 1215, kings were obliged to ask in advance before they would take anyone's money. Nevertheless, the Magna Carta was in essence a baronial and feudal document and did not project an extension of democracy to a wider section of the population.

It's unlikely that democracy would have evolved in England had it not been for the many revolutionary inventions that surfaced and were applied in England in the modern period of history. In the 1500's, people in England, for the first time, had access to a variety of inventions such as astrolabe and compass, caravel, gunpowder, printing press, banking system, weights and measurements, and more. These inventions served as a major impetus to the emergence of an aggressive and viable merchant class, which was destined to set the basis for a novel market and exchange economy. Application of inventions by the merchants led to trade on a scale that was never seen before; as a result, towns, cities, economic growth and expansion followed.

Apart from the Petition of Rights (1628), which specified certain liberties for English subjects, the real turning point in the struggle for parliamentary democracy and freedom was the English revolutionary period involving three civil wars between 1642 and 1651. In essence, it was a struggle between the feudal nobility, who sought to preserve feudalism and the old way of life, and the ascending parliamentary forces, led by Cromwell and supported by merchants, who were looking forward to the realization of an expanding mercantile economy and embryonic capitalism. Royalty, nobility and clergy were committed to the preservation of traditional feudal institutions, while the emerging merchant class envisaged and promoted development of new institutions, based on a modern market economy and the profit motive. The deciding factor which enabled Oliver Cromwell and the parliamentary movement to defeat the nobility and royalty, was the financial and logistical support provided by the merchant class. It's doubtful if Cromwell would have been able to build his professional army and attain victory for Parliament without the financial assistance from the merchant class.

Cristopher Hill interpreted the English civil war as a bourgeois revolution. He had this to say: "The civil war was a class war, in which despotism of Charles I was defended by the reactionary forces of the established church and conservative landlords. Parliament beat the king because it could appeal to the enthusiastic support of the trading and industrial classes in town and countryside, to the yeomen and progressive gentry, and to wider masses of the population whenever they were able by free discussion to understand what the struggle was about."[97]

The English civil war ultimately culminated in the Glorious Revolution of 1688, which led to the Bill of Rights in 1689. The Bill of Rights placed into law certain rights and liberties such as a requirement for regular elections, separation of powers, no taxation without Parliament approval and rules for freedom of speech in Parliament, limited and defined powers of the monarch and the termination of royal absolutism.

The Bill of Rights was a historic milestone and the culmination of the English Revolution of 1642-1651. The English Bill of Rights served as a model for the American Bill of Rights in 1789, although France also exerted some influence on the American constitution. Interestingly, the English model also served as a basis for the UN Declaration of Human Rights (1948) as well as for the European Convention on Human Rights (1950).

---

97   Hill, Christopher. *The English Revolution, 1640*. Lawrence and Wishart, 1940.

Indisputably, the English Bill of Rights had an enormous impact on democratic development, human rights and freedom in the Western world. However, it's unfortunate and regretful that the leadership of the three democratic nations—England, the United States and Canada—lacked the foresight and commitment to develop democratic thinking to a higher level. There is ample evidence to indicate that England in the 18th, 19th and 20th centuries was overly preoccupied with its imperial ventures, building and consolidating its Pac Britannica. The British capitalist class and its power structure clearly revealed its priority; empire building and imperial expansion was to take precedence over furthering the development of democracy and human rights in the nation. England found itself in a quagmire: on the one hand, England professed to be Christian and democratic; on the other hand, it was subjugating people in its colonial empire to vile exploitation and enslavement. The historical consequence of England's empire building has placed the onus on current leadership for developing national democratic institutions appropriate for the new millennium.

It is equally true for the United States, although it reveals a rather short memory when the meaning of democracy, human rights and freedom are being considered. By the early part of the 19th century, not only did the United States embark aggressively on imperial policies, but it engaged in the notorious transatlantic slave trade. More so, there exists ample evidence exemplifying American genocidal policies used domestically against the American Indigenous peoples.

Canada can be excused from participating in imperial ventures since Canada was itself a victim of British colonialism. However, in post-Confederation Canada, Sir John A. MacDonald and his Conservative government cannot be absolved from labelling Indigenous peoples "savages", and more so, engaged in

promoting policies of racism and genocide.[98] Both Conservative
and Liberal leadership since Confederation (1867), might have
utilized their time better by developing a more substantive
understanding of contemporary Canadian democratic institutions and how they can be improved.

Several centuries have elapsed since the historic English
Bill of Rights. One can posit the view that there was more than
enough time to develop a positive understanding of the meaning of majoritarian democracy. The human rights principles
articulated by John Locke (1632-1704), and the doctrine of private enterprise and the invisible hand extolled by Adam Smith,
cleared the path for capitalist development. In the process, a
better understanding of the growth of substantive democracy
and freedom was left for later development.

While exponential growth of technology enabled capitalist institutions, in particular oligopolies, monopolies, oligarchies and multinational corporations, to unfold dramatically,
democracy and human rights were being threatened by corporate power structures at the same time. In his farewell speech,
Eisenhower pointed out the imminent danger to American
democracy, posed by the American power structure. Existence
of entrenched power structures of all three nations—England,
the United States and Canada—is an indisputable reality. The
power structures are subtly disguised and fall under the cloak
and ideology of neoliberalism.

Noam Chomsky, a world renowned linguist and philosopher characterizes neoliberalism in the following way: "Instead
of citizens, it produces consumers. Instead of communities, it
produces shopping malls. The net result is an atomized society
of disengaged individuals who feel demoralized and socially
powerless. In sum, neoliberalism is the immediate and foremost enemy of genuine participatory democracy, not just in the

United States but across the planet, and will be for the foresee-able future".[99]

Noam Chomsky goes on to say that neoliberalism engages in an organized system of propaganda to instill and inculcate values of larger society (i.e. values of corporate capitalism). Chomsky states: "The mass media serves as a system for communicating messages and symbols to the general populace. It is their function to amuse, entertain and inform, and to inculcate individuals with the values, beliefs, and codes of behaviour that will integrate them into the institutional structures of the larger society. In a world of concentrated wealth and major conflicts of class interest, to fulfill this role requires systematic propaganda".[100]

According to many analysts and observers of power structures, a tiny minority in all three nations mentioned works persistently via the power of wealth to impose its corporate agenda on the public. Under the guise of neoliberalism, the tiny power structure is determined to dismantle government regulations, abolish any viable social programs, arrest any minimum wage increases, promote as much privatization as possible, and prevent the unfolding of any environmental programs.

Unfortunately, neoliberalism posits and adheres to the questionable view that such issues and negative values as unemployment, poverty, inequality, human greed, racism, wars and imperialism are features of modern societies and will tend to stay with us.

Humanity needs to come to grips with the two major existential threats facing the planet in the new millennium. It must be said, if there ever were a time for working people and ordi-

---

99   Brown, Justin. "60 Noam Chomsky quotes that will make you question everything about society." Ideapod, 2019. https://ideapod.com/35-noam-chomsky-quotes-will-make-question-everything-society/.

100   Ibid.

nary folk from all walks of life to get together and make a sustained effort to curb the policies of neoliberalism and its stand on the two critical issues, *the time is now.*

CHAPTER 12

The Quest for Human Values

Few people would have the effrontery to say that we live in a safe and stable world. We are constantly exposed to horrifying and frightening events, including increasing natural disasters. Ordinary folk, as well as scholars, continue to express concern of the turbulence and instability being displayed worldwide by the forces of nature. Earth is manifesting various disruptions, from frequent cyclones, volcanoes, earthquakes, tornadoes to certain parts of the world experiencing worrisome drought.

Many people are perplexed and wonder if nature isn't trying to tell the human species something. Could it be that the modern world, with its advanced technology and aggressive consumerism, are gravely disrupting the balance of nature? It's widely known that the planet is facing two existential threats: firstly, a major disaster could occur stemming from climate change; and secondly, the possibility that a nuclear war could precipitate a catastrophic holocaust. So far, the world has been exposed to considerable sabre-rattling; the Doomsday Clock is registered at three minutes to midnight, but the planet continues to spin along. Fortunately, we've not had a major cataclysm since World War II, when the United States dropped two devastating atomic bombs on Japan, presumably to end the war sooner. However, common sense tells us that the instability in the Middle East does not bode well for the human species to secure durable world peace and improve its opportunity for survival.

Shortly after World War II ended, the United States parted with the Monroe Doctrine and assumed the challenge of experiencing a new global hegemonic role. The Christian and democratic principles which the United States claims to believe in and adhere to did not deter it from engaging in imperial wars and conflicts. Post-World War II, the United States became entangled in a number of foreign conflicts and small scale wars, based on the motivation to secure resources, as well as geopolitical considerations. To secure its objectives, the United States and its power structure based its foreign policy on toppling regimes antagonistic to American national interest. The US has been involved in Vietnam, Iraq, Libya, Syria and is now in the 18th year of continuing war in Afghanistan. It remains to be seen how the United States resolves its differences with Venezuela and Iran.

Analysts and informed observers have a great challenge before them in trying to rationalize and provide clarity to American foreign policy. What appears to be abundantly clear is that United States has abandoned its Christian and democratic principles. Surveys have shown that roughly 60% of American people are opposed to the imperial wars being conducted; yet the American power structure continues its imperial military ventures.

Humanity finds itself in a dangerous historic epoch. American leadership, under the influence of the military-industrial complex, appears to have espoused imperialism and the inevitability of war as a dominant value in its foreign policy. What's of concern is that President Trump and his Secretary of State, Michael Pompeo, are constantly sabre-rattling, whether it be with Iran or lately with Venezuela. It appears quite blatant that the Trump Administration, in conjunction with the MIC, are strategizing to impose its aggressive "imperial value" on American people. What's hopeful is that the newly-elected congress (2018) has many astute people, who are challenging and exposing the negative foreign policy of the Trump administration.

Concerning the issue of climate change, Trump took a highly controversial step by abandoning the Paris Climate Accord and calling it a "hoax". It's fair to question, since Prime Minister Trudeau accommodated Trump by arresting a Chinese corporate official, Meng Wanzhou, on what appears to be a trumped-up charge, whether he will use some of his leverage to change Trump's stance on climate change.

However, Trudeau is himself a victim of a Canadian power structure, which exerts great influence on his thinking and value system. Clearly, neither Trump nor Trudeau are on the side of genuine peace—both have approved the sale of armaments to war-mongering nations. The United States delivered a huge armaments package to the monarchical regime of Saudi Arabia, as did Justin Trudeau. Prime Minister Trudeau approved a $15 billion armaments contract to Saudi Arabia, with minimal debate in the House of Commons. It's common knowledge that all four Western democracies and Christian nations—England, France, the United States and Canada—at one time or another provided the Saudi regime with military hardware, which is used in Yemen to murder innocent civilians, women and children. Western democracies subscribe to neoliberalism, an ideology which propagates values inimical to peace and human survival. Neoliberalism delivers its message in a subtle and propagandistic way by saying such negative values as human greed, racism, imperialism, wars, inequality, poverty and unemployment have always existed and will continue to exist.

Fortunately for humanity, there exists a core set of values which counter the negative, destructive and inhumane values propagated by neoliberalism and its corporate media. A positive set of humane core values can be articulated: struggle for world peace, greater economic and social equality, participatory and substantive democracy, concerted control over environment and

green house gas emissions and provision of cultural effervescence for the public.

Let's examine these values briefly:

Struggle for world peace: A peaceful world is desirable
and feasible; wars are anathema and despicable. Humanity is
facing a serious existential threat—the possibility of nuclear
conflagration resulting in an unimaginable holocaust. Currently,
nine nations have possession of nuclear weaponry. Peace-loving
people and all those who wish to preserve and save Earth are
confronted with a formidable challenge. They must find a way of
convincing major nuclear, and non-nuclear nations, for a cessation of any further nuclear and missile testing. Halting missile
testing opens the door for nations, large and small, to work for
an agreement on total world disarmament, to be accompanied
by a comprehensive and verifiable inspection system.

Greater economic and social equality: Western
democracies, under the influence of neoliberalism, are clear and
unequivocal on the issue of economic and social equality. They
argue that any attempt to implement more equality is counterproductive, wishful thinking and unattainable. Inequality
existed for more than five centuries under the capitalist system
and will remain unabated. Neoliberalism attempts to justify
economic inequality by asserting that decreasing or eliminating
inequality will tend to destroy human initiative and the desire
of people to propel the economy forward. It's argued further that
the profit motive under capitalism promotes economic growth
and prosperity.

Arguments put forth by neoliberalism sound attractive in
theory, but hit a dead end in practice. The harsh reality is that
corporations in the course of productivity via the profit motive
accumulate excessive capital. Concentration of wealth and capital at the top of the economic pyramid inevitably results in the
diminution of purchasing power below. In essence, neoliberalism, private enterprise and capitalism cannot resolve the basic
contradiction in productivity—the perpetual dilemma of find-

ing markets for the surplus commodities. This ultimately causes widespread economic and social inequality, unemployment and poverty, which leads to conflict and uncertainty. In effort to resolve the dilemma faced by capitalism, it would appear to be necessary for workers to exercise substantive democratic control over corporate industry, and move society in the direction of operating industry and various economic institutions as self-directed enterprises.

Popular, participatory and substantive democracy: Since the Bill of Rights, democracy in the Western world evolved considerably but not sufficiently to satisfy citizenry in society. A level in the evolution of democracy arrived where changes are required in the democratic process, including changes in the Charter of Rights, which was adopted by the Pierre Trudeau government in 1982. Professor Michael Mandel stated the following: "The meaningless phrases in the Charter were willfully and outrageously manipulated by highly political judges who feigned independence but were actually in cahoots with the country's wealthy elites."[101]

Professor Mandel alleged that the Charter had utterly undermined the Canadian political system, that it was essentially a disguised anti-democratic shell projected as a test of equality and human rights. He argued that the Charter had subtly emasculated Canada's political and democratic system. According to Mandel, provisions in the Charter accorded the judges decision-making rights that ought to belong in a democracy to elected officials.

The key element weakening Canadian democracy is the role played by big money in the decision-making process. Eliminating moneyed interests from the democratic process, implementing proportional representation and closing tax loopholes and

---

101   Mandel, Michael. *The Charter of Rights and the Legalization of Politics in Canada.* Toronto: Wall and Thompson, 1989.

tax havens for the wealthy will enable society to move in the direction of participatory, popular and substantive democracy. Ultimately, in effort to subdue plutocracy, workers in industry will need to exercise greater control over the means of production and distribution. Greater control of industry by workers will likely promote widespread democratization, which will become the norm for more popular and participatory democracy, much to the dismay and discomfort of neoliberalism.

Climate change and environmental sustainability: Much of humanity agrees with the observation that the environment is being raped and the planet abused. The scientific community is in agreement that climate change, greenhouse gas emissions and pollution are a major existential threat facing humanity. Increasingly, new signs keep emerging, indicating that the planet and nature are moving closer to a tipping point. For example, it was recently announced on television that one million species of assorted life are in danger of extinction. In sum, humanity needs to act promptly, wisely and decisively if the suicidal course the world is on now is to be averted.

Public cultural effervescence: A society based on popular and participatory democracy will likely create favourable conditions for the development of human cultural effervescence. As the core set of positive human values become more firmly entrenched, necessary conditions will likely emerge, allowing people to effervesce culturally. The trillions of dollars wasted on destruction and war will be diverted to peaceful purposes and cultural effervescence.

In sum, the positive and humane set of core values outlined above are an antidote to the values advocated and propagandized by neoliberalism and the corporate elite. Whether neoliberalism and its followers will realize the gravity of the two existential threats facing humanity, and will move in the direction of rational thinking, remains to be seen. Nobody can foretell the future, but one thing is clear: inaction by humanity will only bring us closer to the end.

CHAPTER 13

Canada's Nationhood – Perplexing and Unique

Nationalism and nation-building gained popularity in the modern period of history, following the decline of feudalism and feudal relations. It's critical to define and characterize nationalism appropriately to distinguish it from ultra-nationalism. It's also important to understand there are two definitions of "nation": the popular definition means "people living in a given territory under one government"; the other definition implies "people living in a territory exercising a common language, sharing a common history, culture and a common identity". The first definition is a juridical or legalistic definition of nation while the second definition is sociological. In a Canadian context, the national government and corporate media propagandize the legalistic dimension and only pay lip service to the sociological approach. The distinction is important in that Indigenous peoples and Quebec subscribe to the sociological interpretation of nation, while English-Canada and the federal government espouse the legal definition.

Nationalism implies patriotism and devotion to a nation, offering loyalty and allegiance to it; it entails having pride in the nation and promoting its dignity. Ultra-nationalism, unlike nationalism, constitutes an extreme form of nationalism; it implies lifting the status of a nation excessively and propagating superiority over other nations. Ultra-nationalism tends to develop into right-wing political extremism, culminating in a fascist ideology. Historically, World War II was initiated by fascist powers who based their understanding and motivation on ultra-nationalism and racial superiority. This led to imperial conquests, horrendous property destruction, millions of military and civilian casualties and untold suffering. Citizens in an avowed democracy ought to keep a watchful eye on right-wing and ultra-nationalist activity.

Nowadays, nationalism and national aspirations are being expressed openly and visibly by a number of societies. Scotland is one such nation displaying national aspirations, hoping to attain full sovereignty and independence. Observation tells us that it's only a question of time until Scotland declares its independence. Presently, Catalonia of Spain is also wrestling with the issue of self-determination. The Spanish government has been reacting quite harshly in trying to quell and arrest Catalonian nationalism and the struggle for independence. A sad narrative is that of the people of Kashmir, who are entrapped by two powers—Pakistan and India—and are being denied the right to self-determination.

Closer to home, Canada is experiencing sensitive relationships with two different peoples who, every so often, surface and openly express their sentiments and their desire for self-determination. Quebec openly and vocally considers itself to be a nation, but a nation lacking full self-determination and state sovereignty. A referendum on Quebec independence was held in Canada in 1995, with Quebec losing by a mere 1%. The Canadian government devoted considerable resources and effort to win the referendum and retain Quebec in the federal system of Canada.

Of great interest is the relationship that is unfolding between Indigenous peoples and the government of Canada. Indigenous peoples are in the process of challenging the federal government of Canada in attempt to terminate the Indian Act, which they consider to be a constitutional anachronism.

What appears to have emerged in Canada are national entities seeking resolution in a new constitutional framework. Public opinion in English-Canada has some distance to travel to grasp and understand the aspirations of Quebec and Indigenous peoples. It should be pointed out that incorporating the national rights of Quebec and Indigenous peoples into the Canadian federal system is totally in keeping with the United Nations Charter.

The phenomenon of nationalism and the emergence of nation states is a peculiar feature of modern history. A brief reference to the evolution of three European nation states—England, Italy and Germany—may cast some light to understand the national aspirations of people engaged today in their struggles for national liberation.

It's unlikely that English nationalism would have emerged, were it not for the widespread emergence of new inventions that swept across Europe in the 15th and 16th centuries. The important array of inventions such as compass, caravel ship, gunpowder, weights and measurements, banking and accounting systems laid the basis for logarithmic trade and economic development on a scale that Europe had never seen before. For example, estimates have been provided indicating that in 1300, there were 69 merchants in England, but by 1600, there were 3,000 merchants in London alone. The exponential growth in trade and commerce created conditions for the emergence of a viable merchant and middle class, which set the basis for the development of nationalism in England. Under Oliver Cromwell's leadership, the parliamentary forces of England, buttressed by the dynamic merchant and middle class, toppled the Tudor dynasty and feudalism in England. The English Bill of Rights was the historic outcome of three civil wars (1642-1651), aptly characterized as the English revolutionary period.

The Italian nationalist movement unfolded two centuries later, under the renowned name of Risorgimento, meaning "rise again". The 19th century nationalist movement in Italy culminated with the establishment of the nation-state in 1870, with Rome as its capital. The Risorgimento was an ideological and literary movement that played a significant role in arousing nationalist consciousness and aspirations of the Italian people.

This led to a number of important developments that freed Italian principalities from foreign domination and united them politically. An important incentive to the Risorgimento came from reforms introduced by France, when it exercised control over Italy during the French revolutionary and Napoleonic wars (1796-1815). The first avowed republican and national group, expressing Italian nationalism, was Young Italy, founded by Mazzini. The society aspired to educate the Italian people to their sense of nationalism, encouraging the masses to rise up against the existing feudal order. Mazzini was discontented with monarchical regimes and continued to struggle and agitate for a republican system.

Another prominent Italian historical figure that provided great leadership for the Risorgimento was Count Cavour (1810-1861). Cavour promoted agrarian improvements, banks, railways and free trade; more so, he inspired the merchant and industrial class in their struggle for national self-determination. Cavour established an active and efficient government, promoted rapid economic modernization, upgraded administration of the army and financial and legal systems.[102]

The struggle for Italian nationalism and nationhood is complex, involving three wars of independence: the first attempt was in 1848, the second in 1859 and the third and final occurred in 1866. Garibaldi played a critical role in the wars; with his fame growing, he came to be considered a national hero. Following

---

102   Dal Lago, Enrico. "Lincoln, Cavour and National Unification: American Republicanism and Italian Liberal Nationalism in Comparative Perspective." *The Journal of the Civil War Era*. 2013. p. 85-113.

the Franco-Prussian War of 1870, Napoleon III recalled the French garrison from Rome, no longer providing protection for the Papal State. While Pope Pius IX remained intransigent to the bitter end, defending the old feudal order and putting up token resistance, he ultimately declared himself a prisoner of war in the Vatican. The Pope lost control of Rome in 1870 and ordered the Catholic Church not to cooperate with the new national government of Italy—a decision which was only reversed in 1929.[103]

It should be underscored that the basis of the Risorgimento movement was the growing merchant and industrial social class which championed the cause of free trade, economic development and Italian nationalism; they saw their future in the nascent and growing market economy and capitalism.

To understand the genesis and development of the modern German nation-state, it is necessary to consider King Wilhelm I, who became King of Prussia in 1861. After becoming a monarch, it wasn't long before he met with Otto Van Bismarck and appointed him as foreign minister. Bismarck's strategic aim was to unify the German principalities into a strong nation state, with Prussia being the helmsman.

As in the nation-building process of England and Italy, where wars were an integral part of the process, German unification and nationalist development also involved conflict and wars. Within a period of seven years, involving three successful wars conducted by the northern principality of Prussia under the leadership of Bismarck, two nations—Denmark and France, including the Hapsburg Monarchy—were vanquished. The aftermath of the Franco-Prussian war witnessed the formation of the modern state of Germany, which came into existence in 1871. The new German nation-state survived as an empire until 1914, the eve of World War I. It should be pointed out that while

---

103 Kertzer, David L. *Prisoner of the Vatican.* Houghton Mifflin Harcourt, 2006. p. 59-72.

Bismarck was a staunch promoter of nationalism, he detested liberalism, democracy and socialism.

Undoubtedly, Bismarck played a key role in unifying Germania into a modern authoritarian German state under Prussian hegemony. The foundation for the birth and growth of German nationalism was the emergence of a merchant and industrial class, which set the basis for a market economy, promoting national economic growth and development. Zollverein played a critical role in promoting nationalism among German principalities. Zollverein was a customs union, consisting of German principalities for the maintenance of a uniform tariff on imports from other countries, and of free trade among themselves. Bismarck took advantage of Prussian railways as well as Zollverein to expand the economy and foster German national unity.

It may be appropriate for those interested in pursuing further the topic of nationalism to compare the similarities and differences of the histories of the three nations examined.

In concluding this chapter on Canada, it's especially interesting when compared to the struggles for nationhood of the three nations previously described. Canada's narrative on nationalism starts with the Seven Years' War (1756-1763) between two imperial powers—France and Britain. With victory on the side of Britain, the colony of New France became a colonial possession of Britain. With the passage of several constitutional acts, such as the Quebec Act (1774), Constitutional Act (1791) and Union Act (1842), Quebec nationalism was accommodated by the British imperial power. By 1867, Ontario's population had risen to a point where a strong demand had emerged for unifying the regions in Canada into a federal union. Part of the concern for unification came from Britain, which was uneasy about the imminent threat from the United States. Following the American civil war, there was some conversation in the United States on the feasibility of annexing Canada. The mere whisper of annexation propelled Britain to consider taking action on unification. Three regions—Nova Scotia, New Brunswick and Prince Edward Island—plus Quebec were brought into the Canadian federal system in 1867 by the British colonial power. Quebec nationalism and the right to self-determination was quelled by some notable provisions in the British North America Act (BNA Act). It's noteworthy to mention, in effort to pacify Quebec nationalism, Britain and English Canadian authorities conceded to let Quebec call its legislature the National Assembly of Quebec.

On the other hand, Indigenous peoples were exposed to untold genocidal cruelty by the newly elected MacDonald Conservative government. Indigenous peoples were denied basic democratic rights and were subjected to the degradation of their culture and systemic destruction of their way of life. Despite the inhumane treatment of Indigenous peoples, they managed to survive and retain their culture. Recently, Canada celebrated its 150th birthday; however, Indigenous peoples responded super-ficially and coldly to the celebration. The slogan expressing the struggle of Indigenous peoples for self-determination—"Idle no more."—signifies the determination of Indigenous peoples to reach the finish line in the struggle for self-determination. In short, over the past 150 years, Indigenous peoples have devel-oped a strong Indigenous nationalist feeling for the right to self-government and the termination of the anachronistic Indian Act.

Quebec has a different historical narrative; it is closely mon-itored by English-Canadian establishment and is being accom-modated. The National Assembly of Quebec reflects the national interest as well as the aspirations of Quebecois. While Quebec lost its referendum for independence roughly 20 years ago by a margin of a mere 1%, Quebec aspiration for sovereignty has not dwindled.

It's reasonable to conclude, when the issue of national rights, as specified and interpreted by the United Nations Charter are being considered, that the three nations in Canada may find it necessary at some point to adopt a modified constitutional framework to accommodate their national interests.

CHAPTER 14

Artificial Intelligence (AI) – Human Threat or Saviour?

What is artificial intelligence? What impact is it having on our lives? Is it a threat to humanity? Society is constantly bombarded with news of artificial intelligence. With new developments, many people are concerned whether their privacy will be invaded. They are also worried how the job market will be affected by artificial intelligence. Is society facing real danger as indicated by the use of drones by the United States for military purposes? In short, will artificial intelligence emancipate humans from drudgery and monotony in the workplace and bring greater benefits to humanity, or is the planet and humankind heading towards a major cataclysm and destruction?

Undoubtedly, AI can assist humans to achieve things which humans normally wouldn't be able to attain. Machine learning linked with AI has come to be known as machine intelligence. Machines are capable of interacting with their surroundings in multiple ways. The disturbing and perplexing question is whether robots are on the path of taking control of humanity and the planet. Researchers tend to argue that a doomsday projection is remote and a long way off; unfortunately, no positive or definitive answer is provided. However, it's been suggested that robots could conceivably take control of society if humans are naïve enough to allow them to take control. One can surmise that humanity would be astute enough to place the necessary safeguard programming in advance as an essential precaution.

We are told that most current AI systems being used are limited to narrow AI, meaning that present AI can engage only in restricted, specialized activity and that robots currently cannot be trained to reason. In other words, if computers are to do what humans can do, as an essential precondition, a vast array of limited AI problems would need to be resolved. Information available on AI research tells us the objective is to get computers to reason, understand language and respond to visual cues.

What's of great concern in the field of AI is the possibility of creating a novel creature—a being that's immeasurably smarter than human beings. It's been stated that human society is at a tipping point, where a machine or robot will be able to reason coherently beyond human capability of understanding. It's scary but true; when robots reach a point where they can evaluate their own mistakes, and make appropriate corrections similar to what humans would do, a major step will have been taken by AI. Unlike the work done by human beings, robots will be able to do the same work but at incredible speed.

The discovery and scientific breakthrough could be a gift or a curse for humanity. It remains to be seen whether the humans will sustain control over the increasing sophistication of AI and the proliferation of robots. Several notable celebrities express concern on the momentous advance of AI—Bill Gates, Elon Musk and Stephen Hawking. There are many robots in use in society today, ranging from the auto industry, to healthcare, to robotic maids; however, the disturbing part about use of robotics are the drones being used by the United States military against so-called terrorism, where many civilians are being killed. It's quite apparent that the use of drones by the US military to target terrorist activities in other nations is a violation of international law; however, the corporate media, serving the American power structure, views it simply as "might makes right".

In 2017, many renowned scholars and social visionaries gathered in California to see if any principles and practical guidelines could be established while humanity is still in control. The two overriding concerns that were being wrestled with were: How can society arrest the present drift in AI-enabled weapons, and how can proper guidelines be established without constraining AI excessively? However, the undecided issue was how humanity can safeguard its future amid the exponential growth of AI and the nuclear arms race.

Michael Bowling, University of Alberta professor in Computer Science, argues that humans need to exercise control over AI, which literally means implanting stop buttons in robots. He uses the analogy that since one would not build an escalator without a stop button, neither would one build a robot without a stop button.[104] Common sense tells us that people must be assured that a "democratic stop button" is embodied in a robot. Ultimately, substantive democratic control must be entrenched in AI research, and robots and carefully monitored. It's utterly disturbing that AI is currently out of control, as exemplified by the robotic drones that are being used by the United States in their war on terrorism.

Prime Minister Trudeau should tell the public who sets the guidelines for AI in Canada. While considerable AI research is done at universities, an unknown and significant portion of research is handled by private corporations. One can surmise that some sort of public control over AI exists at universities; however, one can only speculate whether any democratic control exists in private corporate AI research. It is disconcerting and worrisome that AI may spiral out of control; so far, no one has made a robot that can fold laundry, cook an omelet or make borscht.

---

104 *New Trail.* Volume 73.1, Spring 2017. p. 7-27.

At a World Economic Forum in Davos, Switzerland, many economists and executives have met and arrived at a consensus that the introduction of new machines, which can learn and act independently, will provide an overall increase in employment opportunity and prosperity. It was stated at the forum that AI is advancing exponentially and is being used extensively by business interests and corporations to operate knowledge-based work activities. Many corporations are in the process of replacing workers with robots. Elimination of employee salaries means a great cost saving for employers, but more so, automated research and data collection saves the corporations an extraordinary amount of valuable time.

It is fair to say that the detonation of the two horrific atomic bombs on Japan in 1945 ushered in a new historic epoch. The use of AI drones today in an undeclared war killing many civilians, is a wake-up call for people globally. As much as we know, drones have not yet been equipped with nuclear devices—we can count our blessings. However, the reality of nine nations being equipped with nuclear weapons does not bode well for the survival of living species.

It would be naive on our part to expect the corporate media to take the initiative in exposing the threat and danger AI drones pose for the human race and the planet. Human decency, common sense, science and logic tell us pointedly that people must become more involved and committed to taking concrete action, compelling the government to establish proper guidelines, ensuring that AI robots have proper safeguards. This means that various interest groups in Canada need to coalesce into a viable populace movement. Interest groups to consider include senior citizens, nurse and teacher associations, peace movements, trade unions, student associations, women's groups and farmers' union.

Alvin Toffler, author of *Future Shock*, possessed the vision and foresight of how human society was likely to unfold when he stated that "the roaring current of change... is challenging the very structures of communities, institutions and nations.[105]

Toffler's observation on societal change is generally recognized. People are beginning to grasp the reality of change, meaning that technology is unfolding exponentially and very rapidly while institutions and human social relations are trailing behind arithmetically and slowly. The widening gap between the two developments are promoting anxiety, confusion, conflict and uncertainty in society.

In sum, the question arises: what structural or institutional changes are likely to take place to safeguard humanity from the onslaught of artificial intelligence? Moreover, is the path of uncontrolled capitalist development and market economy destined to continue; or are we about to witness the emergence of human sanity and a new form of society exhibiting a set of humane values and egalitarian institutions?

---

105   "Alvin Toffler, Author of 'Future Shock', Dies at 87." *The New York Times.* June 29, 2016. https://www.nytimes.com/2016/06/30/books/alvin-toffler-author-of-future-shock-dies-at-87.html.

CHAPTER 15

Canada – Victim of Confusion and Uncertainty

C anadians in all walks of life seem to be experiencing aspects of confusion, anxiety, anger or uncertainty. Whenever the TV is turned on, people are exposed to a barrage of negativity—violence, wars, crime and consumerism. If it's not sexual harassment and misconduct by celebrities, or sexual overtures in the workplace, it's the horrific killings in the Middle East. One needn't be a psychologist to know the impact that violence has on the psyche of people.

Apart from violence, consumerism is having a profound effect on the thinking and psychology of individuals. Commercial advertising on TV is undoubtedly shaping the wants of people to a point where it is distorting their personality. People are being hooked on consumption, not realizing that material aggrandizement may not be the road to well-being, contentment and happiness. It's unfortunate and depressing to witness the onslaught of TV advertising by auto, drug and food industries. There is every type of food one desires, a pharmaceutical drug available for every conceivable ailment and an earth-shattering automobile ready to satisfy everyone's dream.

Extensive research has been done on conditions affecting the development of well-being—whether a person is well adjusted, content and happy. With the economy on the rise, we should be getting happier, but it seems we aren't. Professor Kim Samuel of McGill University argues that growth in the economy (GDP) does not necessarily reflect in human happiness. His contention is that society "requires better measures than GDP for national progress."[106]

According to results released by Gallup research agency, while people smile, laugh and express feelings on a regular basis, the trend over an extended period of time indicates a significant increase in human negativity—humans tend to display worry, anger, sadness and stress. There is reason to believe that anxiety, stress, confusion and uncertainty are serious issues in Canadian society. Studies indicate that people are experiencing negative feelings at a record level.

How do you rationalize the rise of negative emotions when people are materially better off than they've ever been? It would appear that material comfort and a satisfactory economic standard of living is insufficient to provide contentment and happiness. So what is it that Canadian society is unable to provide to allow for the unfolding of happiness in the individual? Interestingly, social scientists and Nobel Prize winners such as Daniel Kahneman and Argus Deaton have shown that the relationship between economic self-sufficiency and healthy well-being is not as closely connected as it's perceived in society.

From observations on happiness, it is fair to conclude that material wealth does not necessarily assure happiness. The fact that a limited and shallow relationship exists between possession of material wealth and the display of positive emotional feelings and happiness is abundantly exemplified by Latin American people. According to Gallup research, Latin American people show the highest rating in positive emotional feelings. A

---

106 Samuel, Kim. "The economy is on the rise. So why aren't we getting happier?" *The Globe and Mail.* May 25, 2019.

logical deduction from observing Latin American people is that social interrelationship, interaction and connectedness may well be the necessary condition for the development of positive emotional feelings and happiness. As John Clifton of Gallup agency puts it, "Latin Americans tend to laugh, smile and experience enjoyment like no one else in the world."[107]

Unfortunately, decision-makers in Canadian society do not focus on positive emotions and the well-being of individuals; on the contrary, the emphasis is on GDP, economic growth and other issues, such as taxation, environment and foreign affairs. Human well-being is rated quite low on the Canadian totem pole, although it should be recognized that Canada has been exercising its initiative in providing some new approaches to the development of human progress. For example, in the 1990's, two Canadian economists, Lars Osberg and Andrew Sharpe, developed a superb index of economic well-being that has gained recognition on the world stage, among other current research projects on improving the well-being and happiness of individuals.

As underscored by Professor Samuel, "It's time for Canada to expand and improve current measurement tools to look more systematically at what makes people happy."[108]

One cannot agree more with Professor Samuel's invocation of political leaders of Canada, to take action on enacting legislation for the promotion of better well-being. Why is Canadian society moving at a snail's pace on implementing appropriate conditions, allowing individuals opportunity to realize positive emotional well-being and happiness?

It would appear that it's necessary to go beyond the rhetoric of politics, which is held captive by the corporate media. Ample evidence and research suggests that Canadians, to a lesser or greater extent, are confused, angry and experience anxiety

---

107 Ibid.

108 Ibid.

and uncertainty. It can be argued, that people are in that state because they are daily exposed to the negative values propagated by corporate media, which reflects the interest of the market economy. In reality, the corporate media, acting on behalf of the market economy and corporate interests, bombards daily the malady of consumerism and ignores the well-being of individuals.

People are utterly confused and have given up trying to understand the basis of violence and wars in the Middle East, which are essentially engineered by the military-industrial complex (MIC) of the United States. It is headed by its erratic leader, President Trump, and supported by a "yes man", Prime Minister Trudeau. People in the workplace are subjected to conditions of the market economy, which generates the phenomenon of alienation. This inevitably means minimizing or eliminating the opportunity for an individual to attain self-actualization, well-being and happiness. As stated previously by Albert Einstein, capitalism has a negative and crippling effect on the individual in the workplace and in society.[109]

It is reasonable to assume the corporate media, acting on behalf of big capital, propagandizes values which are inimical to the well-being of individuals. By examining conditions in society, it becomes quite evident that corporations extol values which gravitate toward war and not peace, toward inequality rather than economic and social justice, show a preference for a limited and not majoritarian democracy and consider climate change a hoax.

 The Canadian power structure, as is the case of the MIC of the United States, is determined to thwart development of positive human values. It's reluctant to work toward minimization and elimination of alienation.

---

109 Einstein, Albert. "Why Socialism."

Professor Samuel is to be lauded for invoking politicians to think beyond the "money nexus" and be only preoccupied with GDP and economic growth. It is critical to identify and expose the forces that seek to perpetuate alienation and negative values which are so inimical to the development of the well-being of individuals.

CHAPTER 16

Role of Interest Groups – Historical Review of Ethnic AUUC Group

I n examining the structure of Canadian society, one is immediately struck with the vast array of organizational groups known as "interest groups" or occasionally referred to as "pressure groups". Interest groups vary in size, objectives, strategies and tactics almost constituting the modern version of factions. They fundamentally fall into two categories: economic and non-economic spheres of interest. Lobbyists are hired by interest groups in effort to obtain concessions from the government.

There are several types of interest groups, ranging from powerful business groups to labour groups, agricultural groups, professional associations and ethnic groups. It's worth noting some of the more important ethnic groups: Assembly of First Nations, Canadian Arab Federation, Canadian Jewish Congress and Association of United Ukrainian Canadians, among others.

However, business groups are the most common type of interest group. It's estimated more than half of all lobbyists serve the interests of business groups. So what is an "interest group"? An interest group can be described as an organized group of people that does not engage in elections but seeks to influence government policy and legislation.

Interest groups are an integral part of Canadian society and thrive in most modern economies. It's important to point out interest groups tend to be polarized in promoting their special interests. Some interest groups advocate and defend business and corporate interests, while others are preoccupied with consumer issues. Still others push for implementation of broad policies on such matters as environment and ethnic concerns. It's noteworthy that the proliferation of some business groups is so pervasive, their magnitude so extensive and the organizational level so sophisticated, that one can posit that they virtually constitute the basis of the Canadian power structure and behave as another arm of government. Examples of such interest groups are the business-financed Business Council of National Issues (BCNI), the Canadian Tax Foundation, Commercial Banks, Canadian Federation of Agriculture, as well as automobile, steel, rubber, chemical and energy industries who may act alone or through BCNI, the Chamber of Commerce or the Canadian Manufacturers' Association. It's essential to underscore that BCNI is the foundation and most important element of the Canadian clandestine power structure. The Canadian power structure, representing the interests of business groups, keeps an eagle eye particularly on issues that may have adverse effects on the corporate groups.

Interest groups reflect different strategies in pursuing their objectives and interests and attempt to influence policy through lobbying, contributions to political parties or by engaging in media campaigns. Successful lobbying to a large extent is predicated on whether interest groups have access to adequate financial resources. Large interest groups are more likely to have the ability to attain their goals as opposed to smaller groups.

The corporate media attempts to keep lobbying in Canada pleasant, dull and controlled. The close relationship of lobbyists to politicians and bureaucrats often results in allegations of corruption and conflicts of interest. The most powerful interest groups (BCNI), the basis of the Canadian power structure, maintain close ties with the governing party. Because the legislative process, particularly policy initiatives, is under control of bureaucracy, interest groups are obliged to express their opinions or provide information to public servants and cabinet.

Western oil and gas industry and Ontario manufacturing industry exert great influence on government policy. It's not unusual for interest groups to engage in conflicts when they do not pursue the same goals (i.e. in the 1970's and 1990's, petroleum pricing pitted the oil industry of the West against manufacturing industries in central Canada). In most situations, BCNI and large interest groups are successful in their undertakings (i.e. they succeeded in preventing an effective strengthening of the Combines Investigation Act, which Trudeau pledged to reform).

In response to public pressure for more transparency and accountability, the Lobbying Act went through multiple changes. An updated Act was passed in 2018, which abolished the Registrar of Lobbyists, replacing it with the Commissioner of Lobbying. The Commissioner is presumably an independent agent of Parliament and is theoretically less prone to political influence.

Interestingly, it has been shown that consumer, environmental, labour and ethnic groups are far less successful in lobbying than BCNI and large business groups. This is largely due to the fact they are not only socially and ideologically distant from the government, but because they are attempting to effect change rather than prevent change. Governments tend to identify with the prevention of change, which is reinforced by the power structure. Moreover, interest groups left on the continuum do not have the resources possessed by large business interests.

There is growing evidence indicating that Parliament and provincial legislatures are having less influence in Canadian politics. The relative weakening of political parties literally means that interest groups tend to play a greater role. With the spiraling cost of election campaigns, political parties are increasingly compelled to rely more on interest groups for financial support

BCNI and other business interest groups provide the necessary funds to conduct election campaigns. In the political context, large business interest groups largely determine the political party that will likely form the government. In return, the elected government caters to the business Interest groups on tax issues and other economic policies. The Association of United Ukrainian Canadians, and its predecessors, Ukrainian Labour Temple Association and Ukrainian Labour - Farmer Temple Association, constitute interesting ethnic interest groups which evolved during the turbulent period of Canadian history.

A few important highlights of the evolutionary process of AUUC will be given some consideration. The origin of AUUC initiates with the Ukrainian immigrants that landed on the shores of Canada at the turn of the 20th century. The first recorded immigrants were Ivan Pylypiw and Vasyl Eleniak - both were peasants who sought better opportunities in the new land and arrived on a steamship in Montreal on September 7, 1891.[110]

Some five years later they were followed by hundreds and subsequently by thousands of Ukrainian immigrants. They came to the new land to escape the oppressive conditions which they endured in their homeland.

It wasn't long before immigrant peasants were attracted to different groups who espoused socialist ideas. A new socialist organization took shape calling itself the Federation of Ukrainian Social Democrats (FUSD). While FUSD grew in numbers it soon decided to adopt the name of Ukrainian Social Democratic Party of Canada (USDP) which took place on January 14, 1914.[111]

The USDP leadership soon realized there existed a dire need for another organization which would embrace a wider circle

110   Peter Krawchuck, Our History, Lugus Publications 1996, X1

111   Ibid p.18

of Ukrainian settlers. Hence, in 1918 a cultural – educational interest group was formed under the name of Ukrainian Labour Temple Association (ULTA) with the aim of accommodating Ukrainian settlers who were not yet willing to join a political party like the USDP. Formation of ULTA gave rise to the idea that such an organization required a temple or cultural educational centre which was soon acted on. The ownership of the building was registered under the name of ULTA and became known as the finest building Ukrainian immigrants possessed on the North American continent. The building has been designated as a historical site.

The world was looking better for left of centre organizations; however, in 1918, the Canadian government swooped down and banned the activity of a number of socialist organizations, including the USDP.[112] Many USDP members were arrested and incarcerated in jails or concentration camps while some were deported. The party was declared illegal and its paper was banned. The political turmoil which ensued precipitated the historic 1919 Winnipeg General Strike, which was a formidable expression of worker solidarity and discontent. It was during this time of instability, confusion and uncertainty that ULTA found it necessary to make adjustments.

Despite the difficult times, ULTA as a cultural-educational interest group, directed much of its attention to the rural communities, hoping to mobilize and attract farm settlers into ULTA. Ukrainian farm settlers were becoming increasingly receptive to progressive ideas and expressed the desire to be in solidarity with workers. Thus, in 1924, at the 5th ULTA convention, many Ukrainian farm settlers joined ULTA under a new name— Ukrainian Labour-Farmer Temple Association (ULFTA).[113] Association branches were organizing drama circles, choirs and

112   Ibid. p. 36.

113   Ibid. p. 38.

conducting regular lectures and discussion groups. It should be mentioned that an important pillar of the cultural activities in ULFTA was the popular mandolin orchestra.

In 1928, ULFTA celebrated its 10th anniversary, showing an impressive cultural upsurge of 167 branches with a total membership of 5,536 members.[114] The ULFTA emerged as a powerful national ethnic interest group to be reckoned with. While the USDP was experiencing illegality, with many members being incarcerated, progressive Ukrainian farmers and workers found a new home in the ULFTA.

For over a decade, ULFTA thrived and prospered despite being often exposed to horrid conditions. Being a prominent left, ethnic interest group aspiring to a brighter future, unfortunately, its hope and dream was short-lived. In 1940, the Canadian government once again descended, declaring ULFTA as an illegal organization.[115] It should be pointed out that although ULFTA displayed farm-labour character, it was neither a communist nor a socialist organization as attested by its constitution.

During 1942-1946, ULFTA was preoccupied in battling the Canadian government for legal recognition and the return of its seized properties. Finally, in 1946, after four gruesome years, the ban was lifted and a minimum of haphazard number of properties were returned. At a second National Convention in January 1946, it was decided that cultural, educational, artistic and community programs would unfold under the name of Association of United Ukrainian Canadians (AUUC).[116]

The role played historically by AUUC is succinctly summed up in the commentary in the article entitled "Toward a Distinct Vision": "while interest groups do not formally participate in parliamentary elections, they tend to support candidates of their

---

114   Ibid. p. 40.

115   Ibid. p. 69.

116   Ibid, p. 80.

choice in municipal and school board elections. The AUUC is no different from other interest groups and has played an important role historically in municipal and school board elections". Further, "As an interest group, the AUUC has an extensive track record, not only in the sphere of cultural activity, but also in social activism, playing an important role on such issues as health care, poverty, unemployment, environment, peace and so on."[117]

AUUC as an ethnic interest group thrived, noticeably engaging in social activism and cultural activities. However, in the 1970's and more so in the 1980's, the AUUC was confronted with a disturbing new reality. While the organization still maintained an active membership and cultural activities were taking place, a worrisome dilemma emerged, confronting the Association. The membership had aged and the Association seemed incapable of attracting new members, especially younger people. According to the commentary in the *Ukrainian Canadian Herald*, "lack of younger people in particular, and the declining membership in general, is the inevitable consequence of the impact of a number of variables: namely, the reality of assimilation, mixed marriages, postwar economic prosperity, the role of the media and television, the lack of a clear vision, as well as the devastating effect of the cold war."[118]

In the social sciences, it's extremely difficult to determine which factor or variable had the greatest impact for the downward trend in membership of the AUUC. However, many would argue that the ULFTA and subsequently the AUUC, with its ties to the Communist Party of Canada, which followed the political line of the former Soviet Party, cannot be underestimated.

---

117   "Toward a Distinct Vision." *The Ukrainian Canadian Herald*. June 2009. p. 4.

118   Ibid. p. 4.

Peter Krawchuk, in his book *Our History*, has this to say about the impact the Communist Party had on progressive organizations: "The Communist Party's control of progressive Ukrainian movement and other similar organizations effectively stifled the independent role, development and initiative of the mass organizations".[119]

Over the decades, the AUUC has been involved in extensive debate on the perplexing issue of how to overcome the stagnation and lack of growth in the AUUC organization. The debate regarding cultural activities and social activism caused some division among the membership; from information available, it still remains a contentious issue.

Regarding the issue of social activism in the Association, the commentary in the article "Toward a Distinct Vision" states the following: "The assertion that the Association can engage in cultural work but not in the various forms of social activism is a classical case of false dichotomy. In the real world of human activity, cultural work to a lesser or greater extent reinforces and assists in the various forms of social activism, and conversely, social activism, far from detracting from cultural work, encourages it and supports it. Any attempt to segregate the two dimensions can only contribute to the further demise of the Association."[120]

In 2018, the AUUC celebrated its centenary, a notable milestone. While the AUUC and its predecessors ULTA and ULFTA made some serious errors and exercised poor judgment on some key issues, it's indisputable that they made, positive contributions especially in assisting workers and farmers in their struggle of basic democratic rights during the Dirty Thirties.

119 Krawchuk, Peter. Our History: *The Ukrainian Labour-Farmer Movement in Canada, 1907-1991*. Logus Publications, 1991. p. 210.

120 "Toward a Distinct Vision." *The Ukrainian Canadian Herald*. p. 4.

Whether the AUUC will be able to inspire its current membership to meet its challenge for recovery and growth in the 21st century, only time will tell. The AUUC Convention scheduled for October 2019 will likely wrestle with the critical issue of the AUUC's future. As stated in the concluding remarks of the commentary, "There is no silver bullet or magic formula that could pull the Association out of its current slump. Meeting the challenge will require a serious commitment from existing membership and friends of the Association in an effort to develop an effective and detailed strategy for reaching out and rebuilding the Association. The Association, while a relatively small interest group numerically, has the resources and the means of focusing its mission and succeeding in reaching out to the communities, promoting cultural work, engaging in social activism, expanding the membership in the Association, and at all times being steadfast in its commitment to the globally shared vision of an "egalitarian global village".[121]

---

121   Ibid.p. 12

CHAPTER 17

The Challenge of Building a Canadian Grassroots Movement

A grassroots populace movement usually involves public participation in a district, community, region or nation attempting to effect economic, political or social change. The objectives of a movement may vary or change, but all movements are consistent in that they all focus on increasing mass participation in their cause. It's important to underscore that grassroots movements are characterized being bottom-up as opposed to top-down in decision-making and categorically reject the top-down command model. At times, the concept of grassroots is conflated with participatory democracy; however, grassroots usually refers to distinct populace movement or organization, whereas participatory democracy denotes a system of governance. Should a grassroots movement attain the levers of political power in society, it's quite likely that participatory democracy as governance would prevail.

Interestingly, there is some talk in Canadian society about the role that a grassroots movement may play in future politics. Conversations are common about how a grassroots movement can mobilize the masses to effect needed reforms which may require structural or institutional modification. Grassroots movements can be geared to mobilize and activate people who may be dormant and apolitical but can be persuaded to become passionate about a cause that affects them.

The grassroots movement is hardly a novel development—history is replete with countless examples of populace movements. Some have been successful in attaining their goals while others failed and became known in history as rebellions or protest movements. A cursory survey of history shows us a number of successful revolutionary movements in the modern period of history (i.e. from 1642-1651, the Cromwellian movement effected institutional changes in England, the French revolutionary movement attained its power in 1789, the Russian worker and peasant movement resulted in the Bolshevik revolution of 1917, the Chinese peasant and worker movement attained revolutionary power in 1949 and, finally, the Cuban workers and peasants attained their power in 1959). There are a number of other examples of revolutionary movements that achieved political power.

There are scores of examples that aspired to win political power in the hope of realizing their goals and effecting the changes they desired. This paper limits its investigation to two historic Canadian grassroots movements and a current populace movement in the United States initiated by the 2016 Bernie Sanders presidential campaign. Two Canadian movements will be examined: firstly, the movements in Upper and Lower Canada known as the 1837-1838 Rebellions, and secondly, the Metis and Indigenous movement culminating in the historic rebellion of 1885.

In reference to Canada, two parallel grassroots movements arose in the 1800's. The reform movement in Upper Canada, and the grassroots movement in Lower Canada. Both movements were first and foremost set to transform the government in favour of more substantive democracy. In Upper Canada, the movement called for responsible government, meaning a government that is accountable to the people, not the king or despot. In Lower Canada, the patriotic movement demanded an elected Legislative Council, as opposed to one appointed by a governor who was the King's representative. In other words, both movements sought a government which would be accountable to the people. Moreover, both provinces advanced the demand that the budget must be controlled by elected representatives of the people.

The grassroots movements in Upper and Lower Canada were taking shape and becoming powerful political expressions of an emerging capitalist system in revolt and opposition to colonialism and imperial Britain. In the mid 1830's, the movement for independence in both Upper and Lower Canada became more forceful and visible. However, to counter the movement for independence, the power structure consisting of rich merchants, colonial administrators, the church and seigneurs of Lower Canada formed a solid bloc, opposing the movement and any thought of independence for Upper and Lower Canada. The merchant class in Upper and Lower Canada (bourgeoisie) constituted a counter-revolutionary force, which was opposed to the movements seeking independence. The affluent merchant class had no desire or interest in severing its connections with Great Britain, in that it derived its power, wealth and privileges under colonial trade. Ultimately, the counter-revolutionary forces, reinforced by British military might, defeated the grassroots movement for independence, which came to be known as the Rebellion of 1837-1838.

Unfortunately, an intense inner struggle in the grassroots movement took place regarding reformism and revolutionary action. While the movement grew, a schism developed between the radicals and the moderates, a historical phenomenon that is unique to movements that become revolutionary. It's been shown there is always a section in a revolutionary movement that seeks to find a compromise and, in the process, betrays the struggle of the grassroots movement.

Leadership of the movement in Upper and Lower Canada was severely lacking. In times when revolutionary action is on the agenda, effective leadership for success is crucial. In critical times, victory or defeat of a movement could depend on the leadership of a few individuals, or at times even one person (i.e. in Upper Canada, Dr. Rolph prematurely started the insurrection, thereby betraying the revolutionary movement). In Lower Canada, the leadership was radicalized over the years, but they neglected to prepare the people for armed conflict. Had the leadership in Lower Canada been prepared in advance, enabling the movement to understand the need for armed struggle, Lower Canada might have established a viable and independent democratic republic, like the Americans did South of the border.

What was lacking was a revolutionary force to lead the populace movement for reforms and structural change. The working class in the movement was too small and undeveloped to lead the movement. Inevitably, leadership of the anti-colonial movement was arrogated by the bourgeoisie. While inhabitants and workers were sympathetic to the cause, there was confusion on issues of political programs and methods of struggle, making the movement powerless because of its equivocation and hesitation. In short, it was inevitable that the grassroots movement in Upper and Lower Canada would be defeated by the opposing forces and British military might.

Unlike the Canadian provinces, which started out as a struggle for responsible government and later transformed into a struggle for independence, the Metis and First Nations movement focused their goal on winning the right to self-government. The group of farmers and hunters, many of them Metis, occupied a corner of Rupert's Land, fearing for their culture and land rights under control of the Canadian government.

With the Dowson-Hind exploration expedition, which arrived from Eastern Canada in 1859 to study the land issue, its recommendation was that the Canadian government should purchase the arable land from the Hudson's Bay Company for upcoming Western settlements. A decade later, the Dominion of Canada purchased the land from the Hudson's Bay Company. Interestingly, neither the Metis or First Nations were consulted about the sale of the land. With total disregard for Indigenous peoples, the federal government dispatched land surveyors, dividing up the land which the Metis and Indigenous held by common agreement for generations. The first uprising or insurrection, which came to be known as the Rebellion of 1870, occurred in the Red River Colony at Fort Gary (today's Winnipeg, Manitoba); however, the insurrection quickly fizzled out with news that Canadian troops would be sent.

The Metis and Indigenous were deeply chafed by the aggressive advance of the "civilizing powers" of the agents representing imperial Anglo-Saxon government of Ottawa. Shortly after confederation (1867), the MacDonald government imposed its notorious treaties on Indigenous peoples (known as the numbered treaties). The treaties turned over the rights of nearly all of the Western plains to the government of Canada. In return, the government made promises to provide food, education, medical help and other kinds of support which the government largely failed to honour. It's sad and very troublesome to say, with the buffalo gone, the desperate pleas for help by Indigenous peoples to Ottawa were ignored.

In 1884, under Louis Riel's leadership, a revolutionary petition was dispatched from the region of Saskatchewan to Ottawa, outlining a number of democratic reforms. In 1885, a new government was declared by the Metis with Louis Riel as president and Gabriel Dumont as military commander. The federal government responded by sending North-West Mounted Police, followed by an army contingent. Battles took place between the federal and Indigenous forces, but the Metis and First Nations movement was no match for the military might of the forces of Canadian government. Comparing the Metis and First Nations grassroots movement to the movement of Upper and Lower Canada of 1837-1838, it is fair to say that the Metis and First Nations movement were less prepared, less coordinated, less unified and didn't show the concerted effort that a movement requires to achieve its goal.

With respect to the emergence of a Canadian grassroots movement, it is worth posing a cardinal question: Is there a need for such a movement for Canadian society? Moreover, what reforms would such a movement advocate at this point in time?

Close observation of Canadian society tells us that the prevailing values are far from being genuinely Christian, humane and democratic. On the contrary, the Canadian establishment, representing the dominant social class, subscribes to and propagates negative views about man and society. Neoliberalism, the dominant ideology of society, cultivates negative and cynical values and considers human greed, racism, empire-building (imperialism), wars, economic and social inequality, poverty and unemployment as natural and destined to prevail for all time.

However, social sciences and research offer hope and optimism for humanity, much to the disdain and disappointment of neoliberalism and reactionary forces in society. Increasingly, people are questioning the authenticity and veracity of the negative values being propagandized by the corporate media. Many scholars and people take the view that such values as peace and prevention of war are achievable, greater economic and social equality is attainable, adoption of participatory democracy is desirable and practical, working out a program on climate change and environmental sustainability is feasible. Moreover, the mythology of human greed can be unravelled, racism can be subdued, empire-building can be curtailed and unemployment and poverty can be eliminated.

Suppressing and ultimately eliminating the negative and inhumane values in Canadian society may appear idealistic and utopian, but a populace grassroots movement committed to positive structural and institutional reforms could meet the challenge by implementing positive and egalitarian values in society.

However, the very thought of a grassroots movement being promoted is anathema to the corporate world and the dominant social class. Undoubtedly, the Canadian power structure, acting on behalf of the corporate world, would tend to employ its hidden strategy to contain an emerging grassroots movement. Should a grassroots movement emerge, it's most likely the Canadian establishment would resort to using resources at its disposal to limit and subdue the growth and impact of the movement. The Canadian government, with the blessing of the power structure, would likely adopt similar type of action employed by Britain in the 1837-1838 rebellion, where it nipped the movement in the bud, denying it the opportunity to organize. Launching a movement when a crisis precipitates is unworkable, counter-productive and highly perilous and risky as a political strategy. It is crucial for social activists contemplating a grassroots movement to be guided by cognisance, keeping a sharp eye open and avoiding any needless provocation. A premature and unprepared insurrection, as shown by past movements, usually results in a disaster and dismal failure.

The real challenge for those thinking about a grassroots movement is to respond to those people who are vacillating on the initiation of a populace movement. They generally argue the time is not "ripe" to launch such a movement and that a crisis must occur first. However, such a strategy plays into the hands of the corporate elite and the power structure, which represents the dominant social class. The establishment (power structure), by virtue of the fact that it controls the levers of force and power (military, police, secret service, corporate media, etc.), is likely to declare a state of emergency, suspending democratic rights and establishing an authoritarian regime—in all probability, setting up a fascist regime. In such circumstances, conflict, instability, confusion and uncertainty become rampant and a horrid state of affairs develops.

It's important to point out when a national crisis occurs, any delayed action in forming a populace movement puts the power structure and the forces opposing change one step ahead of the grassroots movement. Hence, launching the movement before the crisis occurs is a necessary condition for the genesis and growth of a movement. The necessary preparation time must be provided to counter the reactionary and corporate forces. Whether the grassroots movement can win in the struggle and wrest power from the establishment and authoritarian regime depends on the level of preparation attained by the movement— more so, how effectively the movement engages in mobilizing and elevating the level of consciousness of the people.

An objective observation of society indicates there are serious contradictions and troublesome concerns facing Canadians— economic, political, social and cultural. The presence of objective contradictions suggests the time may be opportune to initiate a grassroots movement. There is no magic formula to tell us when the grassroots movement should be launched; however, capitalizing on science, logic and common sense suggest it's not only desirable and necessary, but an opportunity is present in the current context of Canadian society, enabling social activists to launch and build a viable grassroots movement.

With access to digital communication channels including social media, a grassroots movement is in a favourable position to mobilize a huge number of its followers with speed and in a way that was never imagined several decades ago.

CHAPTER 18

Canadians Grappling with a Sustainable Retirement System

The number of seniors in the three nations of Canada, Indigenous peoples (First Nations, Metis and Inuit), Quebec and English-Canada is noticeably on the rise. As Canadians age, we are told that more of us are moving into our senior years financially ill-equipped to adequately provide necessities when our working days are terminated. New statistics tell us poverty among seniors is ascending again, after having experienced nearly two decades of decline. Economic scholars tell us Canada ought to be prepared for a bleak future, meaning that more seniors will be living in poverty and unlikely to rise above it.

Seniors have played and continue to perform an important role in Canadian families, communities and places of work, adding substantially to the Canadian economy and national prosperity. It's generally understood that a high quality of life for seniors depends largely on how active, engaged and informed they are. Seniors increasingly want to remain active in the workplace for a number of reasons, including the idea of receiving additional income. It's well-founded that Canadians have longer and healthier lives than previous generations.

It's understandable that today's seniors are exposed to more choices in their living, work opportunities and retirement.

Records show that seniors', aged 75 and older, participation in sports or recreational activities, as well as in cultural, educational or hobby organizations increased substantially.[122] The participation rate of seniors in service clubs also increased considerably.

For some time, the Conservative and Liberal governments have been providing a range of programs and policies in effort to meet the needs of seniors—keeping them in active lifestyles, having them continue to be engaged in communities and be well-informed about services and benefits available. However, government benefits and private savings will hardy be sufficient on their own to enable seniors to thrive through their retirement years. It is essential that workplace savings must also play a role for retirement; in fact, it should be mandatory and enacted in legislation. It's incumbent on policy-makers to implement the foundation for a more functional workplace pension coverage— a system that provides a stable income in retirement for all Canadians. Canada's largest pension investors, in collaboration with government, need to use their knowledge and experience to develop additional workable solutions. It should be noted that the Minister of State (Seniors) continues to work with departments and agencies of federal government, as well as with other levels of government and stakeholders.

A noticeable observation of Canada's population is that it's in the midst of a fundamental shift. The number of seniors is growing more rapidly than any other segment of population. It's been estimated that by 2041, roughly 25% of Canada's population will be seniors. We are told that in 2014, over 6 million Canadians were aged 65 years or older, representing 15.6% of Canada's population. Further, by 2030, seniors will number over

---

122 "Action for Seniors Report." Government of Canada. 2014. https://www. canada.ca/en/employment-social-development/programs/seniors-action-report. html.

9.5 million people, accounting for 23% of Canadians.[123] The fact remains that Canadians are aging, as indicated by most recent demographic projections, estimating that 1 in 5 Canadians will be 65 years or older in 2024.[124]

It's interesting to chat about the retirement years of seniors and the occasional comments made about the golden age which they presumably experience; however, it's also worth mentioning the various problems and challenges in life they experience.

According to Statistics Canada, 12.5% of Canadian seniors now live in poverty; between 2014-2017, 75,000 more seniors became low-income. According to the Broadbent Institute, seniors are becoming low-income at a faster rate than the rest of the population. Single seniors and women, in particular, are vulnerable in that only one income is provided—no spouse is available to assist. The reality of seniors living in poverty or on low income is that they are not in a position to reverse the situation. In an effort to cope with poverty, many seniors re-enter the labour force (i.e. from 1997-2010, over 300,000 seniors entered the labour force).[125] For some seniors, joining the labour force and postponing retirement is a matter of choice; however, for countless other seniors, it's a matter of necessity and desperation.

Unfortunately, seniors who lack an acceptable and proper income are denied the opportunity to participate in societal activities, which means there is less spending in the economy. The result is that seniors with low income tend to rely heavily on government benefits, which is costly to the government. However, it's important to point out that ultimately the benefits

123 *Government of Canada Report.* Statistics Canada.

124 HOOPP. "Healthcare of Ontario Pension Plan, Annual Report." August 2017. https://hoopp.com/docs/default-source/investments-library/annual-reports/2017annualreport.pdf.

125 *Government of Canada Report.* Statistics Canada.

paid out flow back into the economy in some form, generating business opportunities and growth.

More often than not, poverty leads to social isolation, which means that isolated seniors are less able to participate and contribute to communities and society.[126] Seniors who participate in various activities benefit from volunteering from the satisfaction and efficacy received by participating. Decreasing contributions by seniors in communities result in a great loss to organizations and society at large. Social isolation has multiple effects, such as loss of social skills, development of depression and anxiety, loneliness, alcoholism, schizophrenia and becoming uncomfortable among people.[127] Social isolation also affects the psychological and cognitive health of seniors.[128] Many would describe the relationship between social isolation and mental health as a vicious cycle. Individuals, seniors in particular, who are victims of the two major traits mentioned, would most likely have extreme difficulty functioning in today's world of confusion and uncertainty.

Further research tells us that an estimated 1 in 4 seniors lives with mental health disorders such as depression, anxiety or dementia. Moreover, roughly half of seniors over 80 feel isolated and lonely, and sadly, men over 80 have the highest suicide rate of all groups. Interestingly, falls by seniors are the leading cause of injury. Equally disturbing is the revelation that a significant

---

126 National Seniors Council. "Report on the Social Isolation of Seniors." Government of Canada, 2013-2014. https://www.canada.ca/en/national-seniors-council/programs/publications-reports/2014/social-isolation-seniors.html.

127 Segrin, C. and M. Givertz. *Methods of social skills training and development.* 2008.

128 MacCourt, P. *Promoting Seniors' Mental Health and Well-Being.* The Mental Health Commission, 2014. https://www.mentalhealthcommission.ca/sites/default/files/Seniors_Seniors_Mental_Health_Policy_Lens_Toolkit_ENG_0_1.pdf.

number of seniors in Canada experience some form of abuse, and unfortunately, many of the abuses remain unreported.

There is a consensus among health authorities that physical activity, eating well, healthy body weight, moderate drinking, reduced stress, good sleeping habits - are some of important health behaviours deemed important for seniors to maintain a healthy lifestyle as they age.

However, the necessary foundation for a healthy body and mind is a sound and viable senior retirement system. Traditionally, Canadian workers relied on Canada's retirement system, a three-prong arrangement consisting of government benefits, workplace pensions and private savings. Canada's retirement income system's three pillars—Old Age Security program (OAS), the Canada Pension Plan (CPP) and personal pensions or investments—provide seniors a basic standard of living in retirement. Under OAS programming, seniors receive three benefits: OAS pensions, Guaranteed Income Supplement (GIS) and allowance. However, it remains to be seen whether previously announced increase in age eligibility for OAS and GIS from age 65 to 67 will be implemented. Interestingly, and of concern, we are also witnessing a decline in workplace pensions (i.e. in 1977, nearly half of paid employees [46%] belonged to an employer pension plan; in 2014, it dropped to 33%).[129]

What concerns many Canadians and seniors is that the CPP plan is insufficient to cover the declining workplace pension coverage. Faced with the reality of inadequate workplace or government benefits, Canadians are forced to solve the shortfall by dipping into their private savings and taking advantage of their RRSPs (Registered Retirement Savings Plan). Many Canadians are disturbed, as reported by Statistics Canada, with the revelation that RRSP contributions have consistently declined from 2000-2013.

---

129   HOOPP. "Healthcare of Ontario Pension Plan, Annual Report." August 2017.

Research by the Broadbent Institute shows that fewer than half of Canadians, retiring without an employer-sponsored pension plan, have set aside enough money to cover themselves for a year in retirement. Without the safety of hefty private savings or a stable pension plan income, increasing numbers of Canadians will likely struggle to meet their basic needs when no longer being able to work. Many Canadians are deeply worried about what life will be like when they retire. According to the research done by HOOPP and the Gandalf Group in 2014, two-thirds of people in Ontario have expressed their concerns about not having enough money to retire. One can conjecture what retirement will be like for Indigenous peoples, Quebecois and other provinces, but one may expect a response similar to that of Ontario.

In short, the future for seniors and new retirees is somewhat bleak and uncertain; it depends largely on how Canadians respond to the issue of retirement, the kind of analysis they do and how engaged they become in the democratic process—and willing to take political action.

So what policies need to be established in Canada to secure safety of retirement for seniors? How can positive policies in support of the seniors be achieved? Providing answers to the questions posed necessitates delving into economic and political analysis.

Canada is officially recognized as a liberal democracy, giving Canadians the right of choosing their representative to government in a free, open and fair election. Interestingly, as revealed by Statistics Canada, over the past 50 years, there has been a decline in participation in elections from 79% in 1963 to 55.5% in 2008. Over 40% of Canadians do not take the time to cast their ballot during elections—that does not bode well for Canadian democracy. It's important to note that seniors with a high school diploma were more likely to vote than people aged 25-34 with a university degree.[130] However, young people are more prone than seniors to sign a petition, wear a badge or T-shirt and display a lawn sign.[131]

Interestingly, during the last federal election, Justin Trudeau made many promises and articulated "sunny ways" for Canadians. He even went so far as to say that he would provide openness and transparency in government. Unfortunately, the results of Ipsos poll released in the first week of September 2019 reveal clearly broken promises.

Based on a 27-country global survey, roughly two-thirds of Canadians today adhere to the view that the Canadian economy is designed to benefit and serve the wealthy and powerful interests. Slightly more than half of Canadians (52%) consider society dysfunctional and fractured; it ascended considerably since Trudeau assumed office. What's surprising and disconcerting is the statistical revelations that a large segment of Canadians (61%) subscribe to the belief that Canadian political parties have little care or concern for people. The lack of concern that political parties have for people is reinforced by the statement issued by Darrell Bricker, CEO and representative of Ipsos. The poll's findings show, regardless which party is in power, the harsh reality is that Canadian public cynicism and distrust of government remains essentially unabated. What is more surprising from the poll survey is that political cynicism has increased under the Trudeau government.

It's understandable why Canadians are becoming cynical about political parties, government and the democratic process. Economic and social conditions have become worse for seniors and Canadians under the Trudeau administration. For seniors, it's a hopeful dream to benefit from the introduction of PharmaCare, providing more financial aid to upgrade skills

---

130 *General Social Survey.* Statistics Canada. February 2017.

131 Ibid.

and training, and implementing a plan that would allow seniors to work part-time while still collecting guaranteed annual income.[132] A sound retirement program for seniors can become a reality, but it's predicated on how seniors and Canadians respond to Canadian political parties and the government of the day. Based on the revelations of political research and surveys, it's somewhat doubtful whether the Seniors Retirement Program will advance significantly unless a workable political strategy is applied. Seniors and senior organizations need to be connected with other organizations from all walks of life and maintain close relations with nurses, students, teachers, farmers, postal workers, trade union workers and others. Without the united action of the various organizations, as expressed by a coalesced peoples' movement, it's doubtful whether seniors and Canadians will be able to realize their cherished dream of a stable and sustainable retirement system.

It's important to understand the claim of neoliberal pundits that Canada is a liberal democracy; however, the gruesome reality is that decision-making in society is based on a top-down command model. Canadian society is carefully monitored by a clandestine power structure.

---

132 National Pharmacare is purported to be a drug insurance plan that belongs to all Canadians. The plan is deemed to be equitable and sustainable, where Canadians can have access to prescription medicines based on their ability to pay, meaning any attempt by the populace movement to tax the wealthy and powerful in effort to allocate more funds for the downtrodden and seniors will likely be forcefully resisted. The corporate media, acting on behalf of big business and the power structure, will utilize its resources to propagandize and denounce the demands of the coalesced populace movement; however, on the optimistic side, while the movement may lack the material resources, it has the capacity to mobilize people numbers, and by that alone, it's invincible.

CHAPTER 19

Canadian Foreign Policy – Time for a Review

C anada's relations with nations outside its borders is complicated, evolutionary and a great challenge in trying to understand and get the full meaning. In posing several relevant questions, it immediately becomes evident how complex and extensive the process of foreign relations tends to become.

- What is Canada's stance and understanding of the Afghanistan war that's been going on for nearly 20 years?
- What is Canadian foreign policy with respect to the conflicts in the Middle East?
- How does the Canadian government view Venezuela and Iran?
- What values does the Canadian government subscribe to in its foreign policies?
- To what extent does Canadian proximity to the United States affect its decision-making in foreign policy matters?
- Has the time arrived for Canada to take a fresh look and review its foreign policy?
- What role does the clandestine Canadian power structure play in shaping foreign policy?

The questions posed are a fraction of the complexity of foreign relations that Canada must endure in its relations with outside nations. While Canada is not recognized as a major power, it has displayed a noticeable and significant role on the international scene. It hasn't been easy, and at times troublesome, for Canada to play an independent role in international affairs by virtue of its proximity to the United States.

Interestingly, while Canada came into existence with Confederation in 1867, it was some 60 years later that Canada achieved full statehood. With the passage of the Statute of Westminster in 1931 by British parliament, Canada attained full national recognition and was accorded by law the right and power to make decisions in foreign policy matters. Since then, Canada's foreign relations have been regulated by the Department of Global Affairs, headed by the Minister of Foreign Affairs, and traditionally the Prime Minister plays a prominent role in decision-making regarding foreign affairs.

Historically, Canada's foreign policies were generally aligned and identified with that of the United States and Europe. Canada continues to align itself considerably with the policies of the former Commonwealth nations. However, the world is changing rapidly, effecting changes in relations among nations.

In examining Canadian foreign policy, three basic elements appear to be the cornerstone of the system—economic interests and development; energy and environment, security, defence; and protection of democracy.

Canada's foreign policy in existence today is the historic consequence of continuing and profound economic ties to the United States. Canada's reliance on the United States is a reflection of its accelerated integration with the US, gaining momentum after World War II. The impact of economic integration is that Canada has been left with a distorted economy; it continues to rely on primary and tertiary industry with a visible absence of secondary industry. Inevitably, Canada became dependent on marketing raw materials to the United States of relative low value compared to the manufactured US imports, placing Canada in an economic disadvantage. Economic integration and imbalance in trade relationships tend to complicate and distort Canada's foreign policy, in that Canada has become an easy target for blackmail.

For example, the December 2018 arrest in Vancouver of Meng Wanzhou, and the request for her extradition by US administration, clearly illustrates the political clout the United States has over Canada. Canada acted as a proxy for the United States, sacrificing its role as a sovereign nation. Economic integration and trade policy distortions placed Canada in a vulnerable situation, making the decision-making process more difficult. While Trudeau deserves recognition for concluding some positive trade deals, it appears he mishandled bilateral negotiations with China and India. More so, he refuses to expose and denounce the Saudi regime for committing atrocities in Yemen. Canada's sale of $15 billion worth of armaments to Saudi Arabia is highly controversial and hardly justifiable on moral grounds. Moreover, Canada has imported over $20 billion worth of oil from the Saudi kingdom that could have been covered by production at home.[133]

Of great concern to Canadians is Canada's policy on energy and environment. The Trudeau government made a commitment to restrict carbon emissions, in keeping with UN's sustainable goals and the Paris Agreement.[134]

Interestingly, Trudeau's efforts were undermined and negated by Trump's withdrawal from the Paris accord. It is generally known that energy is Canada's largest and most important export.[135] Canada has been selling its heavy oil from Western

---

133 "Canadian International Trade Database." Statistics Canada.

134 United Nations Framework Convention on Climate Change. "The Paris Agreement." 2015. https://unfccc.int/process-and-meetings/the-paris-agreement/the-paris-agreement.

135 "Canada's State of Trade and Investment Updated." Global Affairs Canada. 2018. p. 83.

Canada, averaging around $15 USD per barrel compared to the West Texas price fluctuating in the $50 price range.[136] Unfortunately, Canada lacks refineries to refine and sell the product, and is compelled to export heavy oil to the US. The United States has become the world's largest oil producer and sits on an abundance of oil and gas reserves of its own with the intention of exporting as well.

In examining Canada's foreign policy security and defence review, it appears to have provided an inadequate plan to meet Canadian needs and its NATO commitments.[137] Moreover, persistent problems continue regarding defence equipment procurement. Canada's defence policy appears to be in a state of disarray. Is it in Canada's national interest to allocate a huge financial commitment for the purchase of new jets to replace aging CF-18 fighter aircraft fleet? Should Canada continue to support NATO, or should Canada opt for a new policy and abandon NATO? The Warsaw Pact, headed formerly by the now defunct Soviet Union, is long gone. Many European scholars and people are questioning the real intentions and purpose of NATO and whether it constitutes an anachronism and is no longer relevant.

Of late, Canada has shown some inconsistencies in its foreign policy, specifically in Canada's military support and training for Ukraine[138] and deployment of troops to Latvia.[139] Even more disconcerting is Canada's denial of "spheres of influence"

136 "Oil Price Charts." https://oilprice.com/oil-price-charts.

137 Perry, D. "Following the Funding in Strong, Secure, Engaged." Canadian Global Affairs Institute. January 2018. https://www.cgai.ca/following_the_funding_in_strong_secure_engaged.

138 National Defence and the Canadian Armed Forces, Operation Unifier, n.d.

139 "Canadian Sanctions Related to Ukraine." Global Affairs Canada. https://www.international.gc.ca/world-monde/international_relations-relations_internationales/sanctions/ukraine.aspx?lang=eng.

for Russia and China. It's quite understandable why Chrystia Freeland would be barred from visiting Russia.[140]

While the Trudeau government can be credited for several initiatives in foreign policy, close scrutiny indicates there are some important shortcomings in his foreign policy. The Trudeau government appears to follow a pragmatic policy, adjusting its policy ad hoc. There is reason to believe that Trudeau consults with the Trump administration on sensitive issues before he makes a decision; the decisions most likely comply with the United States.

Will the next Prime Minister set a new path in foreign policy for Canada? Will they commit themselves to a review and revert to a policy of substantive peacekeeping initiated by Lester B. Pearson in the late 1950's, where he opened up a multilateral role for Canada in international peacekeeping?[141]

Canada is considerably integrated, not only in bilateral economic relations with the United States, but also in security arrangements, as exemplified by the bilateral North American Air Defence (NORAD) as well as the multilateral North Atlantic Treaty Organization (NATO).

Notwithstanding its relationship with the United States, Canada is confronted with the formulation of policies with a number of other nations. With respect to China, how does Canada respond to China's extensive project known as the "Belt and Road Initiative", designed to revive the old Silk Road trade route over land and sea?[142] The Middle East, Palestine and

---

140 Blinsky, A. "Why is Canada's Top Diplomat, Chrystia Freeland, Barred from Russia"? *Global News*. January 12, 2017.

141 Morgenthau, H.J. *Politics Among Nations: The Struggle for Power and Peace*. NY Knopf, 1948.

142 "Belt and Road Initiative." World Bank Group. March 29, 2018. https://www.worldbank.org/en/topic/regional-integration/brief/belt-and-road-initiative.

Iran in particular, necessitates some careful deliberation and planning in foreign policy. In South America, Venezuela seems to pose a threat to the United States and requires resolution. It should be pointed out that the Middle East conflicts have created a massive and turbulent refugee crisis, which does not bode well for the West and Canada.

The foreign policy issue that is getting some attention centres on the question: Has the time not arrived for a thorough, well-planned, deep examination and review of Canada's foreign policy? There was a shift in foreign policy headed by John Manley in late 2000, which signalled that timing was appropriate for a fresh look at Canadian foreign policy. The objective was to establish a better balance in pursuit of interests and values, between bilateral and multilateral arrangements. Necessarily, it implied that basic cooperative relations were to be solidified with the United States as a top foreign policy priority. It's likely a policy review may reveal that Canada needs to pursue a different path, necessitating Canada's reduction of its dependence on the United States, as well as prioritizing other key bilateral agreements with G-7 nations including Mexico, Brazil and China.

Lastly, after a long period of procrastination and delay, the Canadian government has finally committed itself to a new peacekeeping role. However, the decision to send an air mission to Mali[143] is being viewed by those who are well-informed as a strategy employed by the Canadian government to enhance its bid for a non-permanent UN Security Council seat scheduled for 2021.[144]

---

143   Fisher, M. "Canadian Mission to Mali: To what end?" Canadian Global Affairs Institute, 2018.

144   Canneri, M. "What will it take for Canada get a UN Security Seat?" Open Canada, 2018. https://www.opencanada.org/features/what-will-it-take-canada-get-un-security-council-seat/.

Keeping in mind the clout of the Canadian power structure and its modus operandi behind the scenes, it's crucial for Canadian politicians to identify the critical elements of an effective strategy for safeguarding national security, promoting trade, commerce and economic development as well as playing a positive role on the world stage. At this moment of history, a time of great confusion and uncertainty, homo sapiens and all life on earth is being subjected to two existential threats: environmental-climate change and nuclear holocaust. It's incumbent upon our political leaders and officials to be vigilant, decisive, proactive and humane. People in positions of leadership, utilizing bilateral and multilateral institutions, need to use all means and levers of power at their disposal to avert the precipitation of the two existential threats. The main goals of the Canadian government ought to be diminishing the role of the Canadian power structure and attempting to persuade nuclear powers to a cessation of missile testing. A halt in nuclear missile testing would logically lead nations, especially nuclear powers, to work out a framework for global disarmament. An agreement on total disarmament implemented in stages and accompanied by a verifiable inspection system would offer humanity some hope for saving life and the planet.

CHAPTER 20

What's Ahead for the People's Republic of China?

It's quite evident that the People's Republic of China is being ruled by the Communist Party of China (CPC), promoting and safeguarding the public and state sector of the economy; however, a distinct sector of capitalism and private enterprise is allowed to thrive alongside. According to Richard Wolff, capitalist nations, in particular the United States, are heading for an economic crisis.[145] The question arises: What's ahead for the PRC in the next decade or two? Observation tells us that the PRC is confronted with a number of serious challenges, which may shift the political and economic trajectory significantly. A number of scholars and observers have expressed the view that China is at a crossroads and a point of inflection, which will be increasingly troublesome for China in the next decade. It's essential to examine China's history in order to project with some accuracy China's future.

It's not suggested that China will rule the world, but that it will have broad and significant influence globally in political, economic and cultural affairs. China's governance is hardly in keeping with the theories of Marx and Lenin. Observation points

---

145 Wolff, Richard. *Capitalism's Crisis Deepens.*

to the fact that Chinese leaders govern and administer their nation pragmatically to maintain stability and a prosperous economy. So far, there is no noticeable rollback of state-owned enterprises or reform of the banking system; on the contrary, there is evidence of a movement favouring the state sector and a tightening of the existing banking and financial institutions.

It is necessary and appropriate to look retrospectively to trace Chinese history in an effort to project what lies ahead for China. From the time of the American revolution (1775-1783), the Qing Empire of China ruled for more than a century over the richest, most powerful and sophisticated civilization on Earth. Not only did the Qing Empire rule over China, but it extended its control and domination of Southeast Asia. It's noteworthy that when the Qing dynasty first conquered its neighbors, it introduced a writing system, weights and measurements and currency, which endured after the collapse of the empire. Moreover, the Qing Empire took a significant step in establishing a market economy, based on commerce and trade as well as introducing monetization and regulation. However, further development of the market economy was stifled by the Confucius steadfast bias against the profit motive.

China's early imperial history reveals that its civilization experienced a cyclical process of decline and revitalization, of ascension and devastation of civilization. The Chinese understand these cycles as being the mandate of heaven to legitimize dynastic rule. The emperor was regarded as the "son of heaven" and was expected to fulfill his obligations by performing his role as a ritual intermediary between the cosmic and the mundane. Accordingly, if the emperor and his dynasty failed to meet its obligations it was considered necessary and justifiable for people to rebel and pass the mandate of heaven to a new dynasty. The last Manchu dynasty of the Qing Empire, which lasted from 1644-1912, was succeeded by the Republic of China following the

Xinhai revolution of 1911.[146] Sun Yet Sen (1866-1925), regarded as the founder of the Chinese nation and republic, promoted nationalism, democracy and socialism. In 1927, Chiang Kai-shek assumed the leadership of the

Chinese nationalist party, soon to be confronted with a Japanese invasion and an internal civil war.[147] Chiang kai-shek and Mao Zedong cooperated independently in the war with Japan until 1945, when Japan was defeated finally with US detonation of two atomic bombs over Hiroshima and Nagasaki. Mao Zedong and the Nationalist forces under Chiang kai-shek's leadership resumed the civil war in 1945, which lasted until 1949, when Mao Zedong and the communist movement attained victory.

Turning to economic development, communist China experienced economic hardships in the period after attaining power. The cultural revolution and the great leap forward propagated by Mao Zedong turned out to be an economic disaster.[148] It's only in the last 30 years that China began to flex its muscles in economic development. With the extensive support of government subsidies, great opportunity opened up for Chinese business and economic development. Informed observers have expressed the view that within the next decade or two, many Chinese firms will emerge and be in the forefront as global leaders in green energy. Private foreign capital combined with huge investments from the state sector is providing the basis for further escalation in economic growth and development.

China is likely to excel in electric energy, as indicated by its heavy investments in electric automobiles. The Wanxiang Group, having taken control of the Chinese auto parts industry

---

146 Abrami, Regina M., William C. Kirby and F. Warren McFarlan. *Can China Lead?* Harvard Business Review Press, 2014. p. 7.

147 Ibid. p. 18.

148 Ibid. p. 2.

and having purchased a number of American auto parts companies, are now in a position to exercise control of the electric
battery industry and the manufacture of green cars. In 2013,
Wanxiang purchased the American lithium-ion battery maker
A123 as well as its sophisticated technology.[149] Another interesting and noteworthy development involves Goldwind Science
and Technology Limited, as exemplified by a Beijing-based firm,
now a global corporation and one of the largest wind turbine
manufacturers in the world.

It's important to point out that both Wanxiang and Goldwind
are private corporate enterprises. Unlike state and government
enterprises, both corporate entities search talent globally to promote their continued development and innovation as corporations. Currently, PRC appears to imitate Taiwan of the 1970's,
which displayed centralized and authoritarian political behaviour but allowed a noticeable degree of market economy and
capitalism.

Interestingly, over the last three decades, private and
state capital became major investment in Chinese infrastructure. Illustrating the scale of investment in China, the Chinese
have opened the world's longest high-speed rail line, connect-
ing Beijing and Guangshou. Even more astonishing, China has
placed on its drawing board a new airport, the world's largest
and purported to be the size of Bermuda.[150] However, a grandi-
ose project started by PRC is the "One Belt One Road" initiative
(OBOR) (also known as the "Belt and Road Initiative" [BRI]),
with a projected investment of $100 billion. The grand strategy
is to connect China with Europe in a web of roads, rail, power
lines, ports, pipelines, fibre-optics and other infrastructure.
Surprisingly, its optional for the United States to connect the
modest American Silk Road (NSR) with OBOR. OBOR consists

---

149 Ibid. p. 172.

150 Ibid. p. 173.

of two parts: a land-based silk road economic belt, and a sea-based maritime silk road. Should cooperation occur between a US-controlled NSR and OBOR under China's control, undoubtedly, it would be a win-win situation for both countries, as well as many others. To date, it has been reported that over 120 nations have joined the OBOR initiative.

Time will tell if cooperation between NSR of the United States and OBOR of China will continue to unfold. To date, the US is only a nominal and small contributor to the OBOR initiative; major investors and contributors to OBOR are Brazil, Russia, India, South Africa and China. Recently, China signed a multi-billion trade deal with Iran and built a railway, giving it access to Iranian oil. China views Iran to be a vital link in the future between Europe and Asia.

Many observers hold the view that China's OBOR initiative is comparable to the US Marshall Plan, which restructured Europe after World War II. It's argued that the OBOR initiative potentially has the capacity to consolidate a trading bloc that will dwarf and overshadow all existing trading blocs, including NAFTA.

So far, Canadian decision-makers are seemingly silent on and uncommitted to OBOR's trading bloc. However, the government after the 2019 election may be best served by seriously contemplating and moving quickly to attain a trade agreement with China. A signed trade agreement would likely translate into a first important step to gain access to OBOR and countries in its bloc.

It would appear that China's economic and technological development is unstoppable; however, a closer look of its upsurge in growth reveals that China is confronted with a number of serious problems and pitfalls in its road of development.

A critical issue faced by China today is the declining supply of fresh water, as well as the rampant pollution that exists in major cities, with Beijing leading the list. Studies indicate China constitutes 16 of the 20 dirtiest cities in the world, displaying

a degraded freshwater system and growing desertification.[151]
On the positive side, China appears to be seriously confronting the environmental problem; environmental remediation
has become an issue of national priority. Huge investments are
being allocated for hydroelectric facilities, solar panels, wind
turbines or nuclear power stations. Climate change and environment are not an issue for debate in China because people
experience climate change daily and believe it. The concerted
approach employed by the Chinese government, with its massive subsidies, to overcome the problem may well surprise the
world in its central goal of becoming a green energy nation and
no longer relying on fossil fuels for its energy source.

An issue that demands considerable attention in China is
the demand for housing units caused by the growing urbanization and migration of people from rural areas into cities. The
increased influx of people into urban areas has placed a great
necessity for infrastructure development, such as fresh water
supply, sewers, schools, hospitals, healthcare and more.

Unfolding an extensive infrastructure program triggers
the need for consumer spending, both in aggregate terms and
as a part of disposable income. Introduction of the credit card
system is helping the economy to some extent, but the need of
more spending is putting enormous pressure on governmental authorities to engage in some type of quantitative easing, in
effort to inject the needed money in the economy. It's most likely
that in the not-so-distant future, Chinese banks will provide the
necessary money supply. In the process, China will likely evolve
a sounder financial system and an updated the banking system.

Complicating China's problems is the vast sum of money
being devoted to military spending. In recent years, China's military budgets have escalated considerably above what appears
to be warranted. The reason for military budgetary increases

---

151   Ibid. p .171.

can be ascribed to the Chinese perception that the United States is an imperial power, with countless military bases around the globe and cannot be trusted. Furthermore, continuing scuffles between China and the US over tariffs in the ongoing trade relationships tend to negate the building of trust between the two powers.

Reflecting on military spending by Chinese authorities elicits a troublesome question: Why is such a large portion of the military budget being spent on domestic public security, as compared to national defence? One hypothesis is the conviction held by Chinese authorities that outside enemies pose minimal threat. It appears that China is more concerned about the potential threat from within the nation. The current protests in Hong Kong will most likely reinforce the perception that the main threat is internal. A second plausible hypothesis is Xi Jinping's belief, which can be traced back to his reliance on lessons drawn from history. Chinese authorities operate from the premise, derived from past history, that Chinese people cannot be trusted. Whether the reported electronic surveillance and censorship will be lifted in the near future depends on how domestic concerns as well as foreign affairs unfold.

Having reviewed briefly the history, economic development and some salient problems encountered by China, the question arises: What's ahead and in store for China in the next two decades?

Two possible scenarios regarding China's future could unfold and both merit further study and consideration. Observation tells us that China will likely continue to function according to the current ideological and world political scenario. The current international arena is far from displaying a harmonious and peaceful atmosphere. What's exceedingly disturbing is Trump's recent announcement of the US' withdrawal from a Cold War-era agreement on Intermediate-Range Nuclear Forces (INF) Treaty, ratified by Reagan and Gorbachev on June 1, 1988. The treaty banned Washington and Moscow from using certain types of missiles. The weapons system is considered particularly destabilizing because the missiles can reach its targets within 10 minutes, giving little warning or time for decision-making, and raise markedly the spectre of miscalculation. The undesirable and worrisome outcome of the US' abandonment of the treaty is that it could ignite an arms race and further advance a horrifying new cold war. Stephen Cohen, associated with Princeton University, stated in an interview that the present new cold war and the renewed arms race is far more dangerous than the previous cold war period.

Undoubtedly, China is watching closely American behaviour after it withdrew from the nuclear treaty. Of particular and deep concern to the Chinese is the fact that China is being denied its sphere of influence in Southeast Asia. Equally perturbing to China are the numerous American military bases, ranging from Okinawa to South Korea and beyond, which it considers provocative and threatening. The present global scenario, forged by the American military-industrial complex as promoted by the Trump administration, is being construed by Chinese leadership as being imperial in nature, chaotic and dangerous.

However, there is some hope, as expressed by a Singaporean representative on a previous Monk debate. When a question arose regarding which nation displays a more aggressive and dangerous tendency, the Singaporean responded by stating the following: "In the last fifty years China didn't explode a single bomb outside its nation; on the other hand, United States since the time of Obama's reign, exploded 26,000 bombs outside its country." So which nation is more aggressive and dangerous— China or the United States?

Two existential global threats—climatic-environmental and the threat of nuclear holocaust—are the basis of a different, preferable, desirable and a more acceptable scenario. It is reasonable and logical to accept the premise that humanity has no choice but to confront the threats head-on. Confronting the two critical issues means inevitably taking on the American power structure. An increasing number of nations are questioning American foreign policy and its sway on the world scene. As stated in the previous scenario, the United States and the MIC is propagating the rebirth of a suicidal cold war and a notorious arms race. However, the volatility of American politics is setting the basis for the emergence of a movement, which can transform American foreign policy towards a new scenario typified by human betterment and survival.

However, the establishment of a new direction for American foreign policy necessitates curtailment of US influence in fostering the development of the cold war and the wasteful arms race. Currently, the United States is fanning the flames of war. It was reported recently that the United States signed a contract with Ukraine, worth $39 million to provide anti-tank missiles. This type of behaviour raises the eyebrows of China.

Hopefully, three major powers—Russia, China and India—will take the needed initiative to spearhead an agreement on world nuclear disarmament. It's in the national interest of all three nations, especially China and India with their huge populations, to promote world disarmament in an effort to abolish the horrendous military waste, and more so, to avert a nuclear dark winter. Should the three major powers attain support from other nuclear powers, sufficient pressure could be mounted on the United States to enrol in the initiative. However, the success of the three-nation initiative is predicated on the emergence and development of a people's movement. Any attempt by nuclear powers and other nations moving toward an agreement on disarmament is unlikely unless a mass people's movement evolves to support the new scenario. A disarmament agreement would logically be accompanied by a sound inspection and verification system.

Today we can clearly observe an era of imagination, innovation and challenge in Chinese business and economic development. As part of a future scenario, Chinese development is deeply integrated with domestic as well as with international markets. Chinese students bring their skills from abroad, aiming to coalesce their education with that of China.

An interesting observation tells us China has once again arisen as a great power. Beijing has become the centre of a new and unique civilization that extends its influence and prominence over Southeast Asia. Especially noticeable and becoming a show-piece worldwide are Chinese designs of economic development, education and various aspects of infrastructure. Incredibly, Chinese language and culture are being disseminated by more than 300 Confucius Institutes in 100 hundred countries.[152]

It's quite conceivable, being a major new player on the world scene, and with the assistance of Russia, India, Japan and European and other nations, China may exercise the opportunity to take the lead and bring an end to the suicidal war mentality fostered by the United States and the MIC. Movement in the direction of world disarmament and the termination of the cold war and arms race would open the door for a more desirable scenario and a new vista for humanity. It would seem appropriate to end this chapter by making reference to Henry Kissinger, former American presidential advisor, when stated that "China takes the long view and sees history as being on their side."[153]

---

152 Ibid. p. 169.

153 Ibid. p. 167.

Bibliography

Abrami, Regina M., William C. Kirby and F. Warren McFarlan. *Can China Lead?* Harvard Business Review Press, 2014.

"Action for Seniors Report." Government of Canada. 2014. https://www.canada.ca/en/employment-social-development/programs/seniors-action-report.html.

"Alvin Toffler, Author of 'Future Shock', Dies at 87." *The New York Times.* June 29, 2016. https://www.nytimes.com/2016/06/30/books/alvin-toffler-author-of-future-shock-dies-at-87.html.

"Belt and Road Initiative." World Bank Group. March 29, 2018. https://www.worldbank.org/en/topic/regional-integration/brief/belt-and-road-initiative.

Benet's Reader's Encyclopedia. Fourth Edition, 1996.

Blinsky, A. "Why is Canada's Top Diplomat, Chrystia Freeland, Barred from Russia"? *Global News.* January 12, 2017.

Butler, Charles Henry. *The Treaty Making Power of the United States.* The Banks Law Pub. Corp., 1902.

Brown, Justin. "60 Noam Chomsky quotes that will make you question everything about society." Ideapod, 2019. https://ideapod.com/35-noam-chomsky-quotes-will-make-question-everything-society/.

"Canada's State of Trade and Investment Updated." Global Affairs Canada. 2018.

"Canadian Bubble Exposed." *Mises Institute.* https://mises.org/wire/canadian-bubble-exposed.

"Canadian International Trade Database." Statistics Canada. https://www5.statcan.gc.ca/cimt-cicm/commodities-mar-chandises?lang=eng&chapterId=27&chapterName=-Mineral+fuels%2C+oils+and+products+of+distilla-tion%3B+bituminous+subs%3Bmineral+waxes&sec-tionId=5&sectionLabel=V+-+Mineral+products&ref-Month=1&refYr=2017&freq=6&countryId=999&usaS-tate=0&provId=1&dataTransformation=0&search-Str=&monthStr=January.

"Canadian Sanctions Related to Ukraine." Global Affairs Canada. https://www.international.gc.ca/world-monde/international_relations-relations_internationales/sanc-tions/ukraine.aspx?lang=eng.

Canneri, M. "What will it take for Canada get a UN Security Seat?" Open Canada, 2018. https://www.opencanada.org/features/what-will-it-take-canada-get-un-security-council-seat/

Canada Without Poverty. http://www.cwp-csp.ca/poverty/the-cost-of-poverty/.

Carrington, Demian. "Green Movement Greatest Threat to Freedom." *The Guardian.* January 30, 2017.

Dal Lago, Enrico. "Lincoln, Cavour and National Unification: American Republicanism and Italian Liberal Nationalism in Comparative Perspective." *The Journal of the Civil War Era.* 2013.

Dalai Lama. Speech at Londonderry. November 11, 2017.

Einstein, Albert. "Why Socialism?" *Monthly Review,* 1949.

Einstein, Albert. *The World As I See It*. Citadel Press Books, 1956.

Eisenhower, Dwight D. Farewell Speech, 1961.

Eltis, David. *Economic Growth and the Ending of the Transatlantic Slave Trade*. New York: Oxford University Press, 1993.

"English Civil War." Wikipedia. https://en.wikipedia.org/wiki/English_Civil_War.

Fisher, Irving. *100% Money and the Public Debt.*

Fisher, M. "Canadian Mission to Mali: To what end?" Canadian Global Affairs Institute, 2018.

Foster, Bellamy, "The Plight of the U.S. Working Class." *Monthly Review* 65, No. 8 (Jan 2014).

Fountain, Henry. "Myron Bell takes on the EPA." *The New York Times*. November 11, 2016.

Fromm, Eric. *Marx's Concept of Man*. New York: Frederick Ungar Publishing Co., 1968.

General Social Survey. Statistics Canada. February 2017.

Giverty, M. & C. Segrin. *Handbook of Communication and Social Interaction Skills*. 2008.

Government of Canada Report. Statistics Canada.

Hayek, Frederick. *The Road to Serfdom*. Routledge Press, 1944.

Heiden, Konrad. *Der Fueher*. Boston: Houghton Miffin, 1944.

Hill, Christopher. *The English Revolution, 1640*. Lawrence and Wishart, 1940.

HOOPP. "Healthcare of Ontario Pension Plan, Annual Report." August 2017. https://hoopp.com/docs/default-source/investments-library/annual-reports/2017annualreport.pdf.

Kalecki, Michael. *The Last Phase in the Transformation of Capitalism*. New York: Monthly Review Press, 1972.

Keynes, Maynard John. *The General Theory of Employment, Interest and Money.* Palgrave Macmillan, 1936.

Kertzer, David L. *Prisoner of the Vatican.* Houghton Mifflin Harcourt, 2006.

Krawchuk, Peter. *Our History: The Ukrainian Farmer-Labour Movement in Canada, 1907-1991.* Logus Publications, 1991.

Langer, William. "A Critique of Imperialism." *Foreign Affairs.* https://www.foreignaffairs.com/articles/1935-10-01/critique-imperialism

Locke, John. *Second Treatise of Civil Government.* https://www.earlymoderntexts.com/assets/pdfs/locke1689a.pdf.

Mandel, Michael. *The Charter of Rights and the Legalization of Politics in Canada.* Toronto: Wall and Thompson, 1989.

MacCourt, P. *Promoting Seniors' Mental Health and Well-Being.* The Mental Health Commission, 2014. https://www.mentalhealthcommission.ca/sites/default/files/Seniors_Seniors_Mental_Health_Policy_Lens_Toolkit_ENG_0_1.pdf.

McChesney, Robert W. and John Nichols. *People Get Ready.* New York: Nation.

Mills, C. Wright. *The Power Elite.* Oxford University Press, 1956.

Morgenthau, H.J. *Politics Among Nations: The Struggle for Power and Peace.* NY Knopf, 1948.

National Centre for Truth and Reconciliation. "Honouring the Truth, Reconciling for the Future." http://nctr.ca/reports.php

National Defence and the Canadian Armed Forces, Operation Unifier, n.d.

National Seniors Council. "Report on the Social Isolation of Seniors." Government of Canada, 2013-2014. https://www.

canada.ca/en/national-seniors-council/programs/publica-
tions-reports/2014/social-isolation-seniors.html.

New Trail. Volume 73.1, Spring 2017. University of Alberta.

"Oil Price Charts." https://oilprice.com/oil-price-charts.

Poverty Institute of Canada, The. https://www.povertyinsti-
tute.ca/.

Perry, D. "Following the Funding in Strong, Secure, Engaged."
Canadian Global Affairs Institute. January 2018. https://
www.cgai.ca/following_the_funding_in_strong_secure_
engaged.

Perry, J. William. Speech at Washington National Cathedral.
2017.

Poulantzas, Wicos. *Fascism and Dictatorship.* London: Verso,
1974.

Rousseau, Jacques-Jean. *The Essential Writings of Rousseau.*

Sanders, Bernie. "To Reign in Wall Street, Fix the Fed." *The
New York Times.* https://www.nytimes.com/2015/12/23/
opinion/bernie-sanders-to-rein-in-wall-street-fix-the-fed.
html

Samuel, Kim. "The economy is on the rise. So why aren't we
getting happier?" *The Globe and Mail.* May 25, 2019.

Schmitt, Carl, "The Legal Basis of the Total State, Griffins ed.,
Fascism.

Smith, Adam. *The Wealth of Nations.* University of Chicago.

Stannard, David E. *American Holocaust: The Conquest of the
New World.* Oxford University Press, 1993.

Sweezy, Paul and Paul A. Baran. *Monopoly Capital: An Essay
on the American Economic and Social Order.* New York:
Monthly Review Press, 1966.

Samir, Amin. "The Return of Fascism in Contemporary Capitalism." *Monthly Review* 66, No.4 (Sep 2014).

"Toward a Distinct Vision." *The Ukrainian Canadian Herald.* June 2009.

Trump, Donald. Inaugural address. January 20, 2017.

United Nations Framework Convention on Climate Change. "The Paris Agreement." 2015. https://unfccc.int/process-and-meetings/the-paris-agreement/the-paris-agreement.

Von Mises, Ludwig. *Bureaucracy.* Yale University Press, 1944.

Wolff, Richard. *Capitalism's Crisis Deepens.* Haymarket Books, 2016.

To order more copies of this book, find books by other Canadian authors, or make inquiries about publishing your own book, contact PageMaster at:

PageMaster Publication Services Inc.
11340-120 Street, Edmonton, AB T5G 0W5
books@pagemaster.ca
780-425-9303

catalogue and e-commerce store
PageMasterPublishing.ca/Shop

Mike with his grandchildren.

About the Author

Michael Uhryn was born on June 23, 1936 in a small town in Peace River County in Northern Alberta. His early years centered in a rural environment and family farm living. After graduating from high school, he attended the University of Alberta earning a Masters degree. After spending considerable time as an instructor in education, he became involved with business, social activism and music. During the Vietnam War, he participated actively in helping to mobilize people, compelling the United States to end its unjustifiable participation in the war. In recent years, he has been actively wrestling with and trying to bring greater awareness to the two existential threats facing humanity – climate (environmental) change and nuclear war. He feels passionately about exposing the destructive negative values being propagandized in society and considers it to be his duty to promote antipodal egalitarian values as humanity is on its long and difficult journey of building a global humanitarian village.